GOING SELF-EMPLOYED

Also available

Start Your Own Business
Internet Marketing –
  How to Get a Website that Works for Your Business
Successful Property Letting

GOING SELF-EMPLOYED

EMPLOYED

HOW TO START OUT IN BUSINESS ON YOUR OWN

Steve Gibson

RIGHT WAY

Constable & Robinson Ltd
55–56 Russell Square
London WC1B 4HP
www.constablerobinson.com

First published by Right Way,
an imprint of Constable & Robinson, 2008
Updated 2012

A copy of the British Library Cataloguing in Publication Data
is available from the British Library

ISBN: 978-0-7160-2188-9

Printed and bound in the EU

5   7   9   10   8   6   4

DEDICATION

This book is dedicated to the brave souls who start up a new business – currently over 400,000 a year in the UK.

ACKNOWLEDGEMENTS

I would like to thank: Mel Jones for allowing her business plan to be used, Clive Elliot for his support and understanding of the self-employed world, Roy and Clare Robinson for their inspiration, Peter Bishop for guidance and, of course, the many start-ups who contributed tips.

And especially, as ever, Cathy, Emily and Aidan.

ABOUT THE AUTHOR

Steve Gibson originally worked in sales, marketing, retailing and wholesaling within the horticultural trade sector. Having worked for two of the leading wholesale nurseries in Europe, he decided to take the plunge into self-employment in 1992.

In 1998 Steve formed Start Business which helped hundreds of people to set up their own businesses. Many more were inspired by the guidance and help contained within these pages when this book was first published in 2008.

Sadly Steve passed away in December 2011 from mesothelioma, the asbestos related cancer. Further information about this type of cancer can be found at www.mesothelioma.uk.com. Steve's family has been inundated with messages from past clients who had received support from him to follow their dreams of starting up a business. They expressed their gratitude for the help, support and friendship he gave them, which was above and beyond that expected of a business adviser.

CONTENTS

TIME TO SET THE WORLD ALIGHT . . .

If you had a choice between employment and self-employment which would you pick? The fact that you have bought this book suggests that you have either taken the decision to go it alone or at least consider it a choice in your life. This is a big responsibility for me, as author – a part in a change in your life!

As a self-employed business start-up trainer and adviser I have worked with a wide variety of self-employed people – over 3,000 of them, and rising. Some succeeded and some failed, though I'm glad to say the majority are in the first category.

But why is one landscape gardener a success when another fails?

I would like to believe that the level of training and advice for both had been similar. Both know their plants and where to source supplies. Both are well trained and knowledgeable. But one makes it and the other calls it a day, licks his wounds and seeks employment.

Working with the self-employed has shown me time and time again that it's not the business idea that will make things work out or otherwise – it's the individual. Couple those individual qualities with a sprinkling of common sense and the willingness to learn from and network with other self-employed people. OK, OK: a barmy idea is always a barmy idea. But the barmy never recognise it!

INTRODUCTION

Tips and Yet More Tips

That's what this book is about: common sense and tips from those that are in, or may be considering joining, the world of the self-employed. And let's make a clear distinction here: the self-employed – rightly or wrongly – often don't consider themselves to be in business. At least, not in business in any academic sense of the word. Rather, theirs is often a lifestyle decision. But, to go back to our landscape gardener who failed, might he have fared better if he had actually considered himself to be in business?

At one point the title of this book was going to be *How to Fail in Business Before You Even Start*. But I thought that was too negative and cynical.

However, rather than theorise about self-employment, I hope to give examples of what worked, and why, for some of those many fearless, self-employed characters it has been my pleasure to work with over the years.

Perhaps you have reached the end of your tether with working for that large organisation? Fed up with the boss who doesn't care? Or does redundancy loom? Perhaps now is the time to create your own empire or get a grip on your lifestyle? People enter self-employment for various reasons. One client said she was 'tired of the neglect of the large employer'.

Whatever your reason, welcome. Self-employment can be

many things to many people. This book, I hope, will guide you through the maze and out the other side waving the sword of self-employment.

(Sorry, I can get a bit carried away on occasion.)

Advice

To some taking advice is a sign of weakness rather than a necessary skill. No one congratulates you for being good at it. When was the last time you were congratulated for 'taking advice well'? In the advice game, we would rather be perceived as the one dispensing wisdom rather than seeking it.
Mark McCormack

1

THE MIND GAME STUFF

Where to Begin?
Well, how about with you? Would you be right for self-employment? Perhaps you have friends who are self-employed and the lifestyle looks appealing. Or you feel you are in a dead-end job with little or no prospect for advancement. The fear of redundancy may make you want to take control of your own destiny.

Well, answer these questions:
Do you like regular holidays?
A steady income with add on benefits?

And, go on be honest: do you find that the odd day when you can look busy shuffling some bits of paper about isn't too bad either?

If you've answered 'yes' forget it... self-employment isn't for you.

Fear
That little darkroom where negatives are developed.
Michael Pritchard

Over the years I have collected some thoughts from the self-employed themselves on what it is like to be self-employed. How do you measure up?

Essential Skills

- **Motivation:** simply the ability to get up in the morning and get going without instructions from an employer or boss. 'Lazy' and 'self-employed' don't go in the same sentence.

- **Belief:** in your product or service. If you have any doubts, customers will sense them and run a mile!

- **Marketing:** of you. No one else is going to do this for you. Sadly, this is an area the self-employed often neglect.

- **Focus:** (or is it vision?) and a clear sense of purpose about where you want to be and how you plan to get there.

- **Resilience:** bucket loads of this will be needed! The capacity not to give up when orders are lost and delays are faced will be essential.

- **Organisation:** deal with those piles of paper. Get your invoices out and be ready to chase when they are not paid. Remember you are not in business to be a money-lender – unless, of course, money-lending is your business!

- **Loneliness:** if you think this should be in the next section, then perhaps self-employment is not for you – or not yet! Linked closely to motivation, there is a different mind-set to grasp: emotional loneliness, which isn't as bad as it sounds!

- **Inspiration:** sometimes just seeking it and looking forward to creating new opportunities.

The Future

What you are now comes from what you have been and what you will be is what you do now.
The Buddha

Beasts to Avoid

- **Over-caution:** learn to take risks and when to stick your neck out. The faint-hearted won't progress. Can you accept that by starting your own business you are a risk-taker? Are you comfortable with risk-taking?

- **Easy target-setting:** while you need to be sensible, fear of failure may make you set your sights too low.

- **Financial motivations:** sounds bizarre, but if you think self-employment is a quick road to riches, you could be in for a rude awakening. Try the lottery or *Pop Idol* instead. Keep cash in sight, but let other reasons for self-employment be your prime motivators, at least to start with!

- **Procrastination:** or, put simply, over-indulging in thinking and planning and never getting on with it. Oh yes – time management for the self-employed is an important skill to master.

- **Butterfly mind:** in other words, one that flits from task to task. Self-employment can offer variety, just avoid all 57 of them!

- **Cul-de-sacs:** a polite way of saying keeping on course and not chasing too many other opportunities. Yes, keep an open mind to new ideas, but without losing focus.

- **Poor delegation:** seeing your business too much as 'yours' and precious to you. Others – and it could be your employees – can help you achieve your goals, so work with them.

- **Not watching the opposition:** it exists and it wants to take your customers away. Keep an eye out; remember that your customers always have a choice. Never, ever fall into the trap of believing that you have no competition. You are too sensible for that surely? Your competition may not be direct. Just remember that customers always have a choice how and where to spend their cash.

Decisions, Decisions

My advice about decision-making is this: whatever you do, don't camp at the fork in the road. It is far better to make the wrong decision, than not to make one at all.

Jim Rohn

Lifestyle

- **Flexible working hours:** you may be able to choose your own working hours or, as the saying goes, 'the self-employed can only work half a day – and you can pick your own 12 hours!'

- **Skills:** this could be the chance to develop or learn new ones. No matter what your background, you won't have all the skills needed to run your own business. Get trained. And don't be too proud to admit you need it!

- **Work from home:** yes, this can hover about in the 'avoid' section! No longer having to commute can be a great boost to your lifestyle. But be warned. I remember one new start-up who didn't get out of his pyjamas for a week. The novelty of working from home became soporific until he realised he had to get out there and sell.

- **Spend time with the family and friends:** remember them? They are important to your business. Seize every opportunity to say 'thanks' for their support.

- **Self-control:** you are the boss, and you will have the chance to start doing things your way.

- **Choice:** of customers and whom you deal with in your

working day. Unpleasant customers and work colleagues can no longer make demands on your time. Actually it's not true, that one about unpleasant customers; you just may have a better chance of avoiding them.

- **Variety:** linked to the last one, but while the self-employed are loners to some extent, you will find your days will become more varied and your circle of contacts will probably grow.

Optimist or Pessimist?
A pessimist sees difficulty in every opportunity. An optimist sees opportunity in every difficulty.
Winston Churchill

Pitfalls to Avoid

- **Your business takes over:** learn to balance your 'precious' business with your family, friends and social life. Your friends will stop asking 'How is the business?' They're fed up with you boring them rigid about it!

- **Health:** watch it, and keep fit. You will need the constitution of an elephant. Take out some health insurance.

- **Survival income:** check this and if the business idea does not provide it, then ask why are you bothering? You want to make money, don't you?

- **Income variations:** the income graph for the self-employed can be, to put it mildly, volatile! That regular pay day vanishes and some customers will take as long as they like to pay. Will you be able to cope with this degree of uncertainty?

- **Unemployable:** the self-employed lifestyle can become addictive. But the more you do it, the less you may become employable by orthodox employers. In short, you will no longer fit the mould, be unable to do as others tell you, or confirm to the rules of the company 'game'.

- **Ostrich approach:** burying your head in the sand and avoiding that nasty phone call, invoice or red tape. They don't go away. Remember one of your motives for choosing self-employment was to be 'in control of your own destiny' – so deal with them!

- **Ego:** status sometimes plays a great role in choosing self-employment. You may seek a certain standing in the local business community and be tempted to buy 'baubles' like a fast car, posh office equipment, perhaps just to impress former work colleagues. Don't – not until you can afford to!

- **Playing at it:** self-employment isn't a game, though if you are going to be miserable doing it consider staying in the world of the employed, as the chances are that you will earn more by that route. So, have fun and get a buzz from it – but take it seriously.

Disappointment
A hot water bottle with a hole – you seek warmth and rest but instead you get dampness and discomfort.
Anon

After several years of helping start-ups I have become convinced that while people can be trained to do book-keeping, marketing, selling and so on, training can only go so far with instilling the 'attitude' of the self-employed.

Often when I ask those considering self-employment, 'Why do you want to do it?', they will answer 'Freedom'.

But freedom from what?

Stroppy customers? Erratic suppliers? They don't go away just because you are self-employed. So is it a mental freedom, or perhaps liberation from boredom? Whatever this freedom principle is I can usually detect it in the glint in their eyes, or from the sparkle in their voice as they describe their business idea. This will be lost on non-Trekkies (there – now you *know* I'm weird) but the employed are the alien race 'the Borg' featured in *Star Trek*. The self-employed, well then we must be Picard. For non-Trekkies the Borg absorb races into a 'sameness'. Their credo is 'you will be assimilated'; well, they ain't met us self-employed yet!

Problems
The man who can smile when things go wrong has thought of someone he can blame it on.
Anon

Why do Businesses Fail?
Many reasons . . . a mix of these:
Credit problems.
Poor location.
No, or too few, customers.
Red tape.
Under-capitalised.
Over-trading.
Health problems.
Family commitments.
Poor management skills.

But one of the biggest in my humble opinion:
Lack of experience.

Don't assume that being your own boss makes you automatically a good boss.

My background is in sales and marketing management. When I went self-employed I thought I knew how to run a business. Well, I knew those aspects. But not finance, administration and all those other skills. When you were employed, others took care of their sections.

Remember – employment is nothing like self-employment.

2

TO BUSINESS PLAN OR NOT TO BUSINESS PLAN?

Why Bother to Write a Business Plan? Is it That Important?
I must admit to having mixed feelings about business plans,
particularly when it comes to a new business. I'm not alone
either. Start-ups will often say that they find the idea bemusing.

It is the figures bit that gets them. 'If I'm starting a new
business then how do I know what my sales are going to be?'
A good point – you've got to give it to them. Sure, when
buying a business there will be figures to go on and the projections will be easier. Perhaps also you will have been running
the potential business on a part-time basis. So again the
projections are easier. I think for any new business a business
adviser would be negligent if he didn't encourage research,
promotional planning and consideration about day-to-day
running issues.

The financial projections? Well, perhaps we can encourage
you to look on it as cash budgeting rather than forecasting.
When you put it that way it doesn't sound so bad does it? The
money bit will be covered later. For the moment we will stick
to a broader view of the business plan.

Unfortunately, too many start-up businesses are put through
a business planning process (by those that should know better)
that is irrelevant, ponderous and stifles the creative process of
business start-up.

Planning Software
Business Plan Software
Don't go and buy business plan software. All the software you need is available for free from your local bank.

One of my favourite business writers, Geoff Burch, has likened the writing of your first business plan to trying to pin a jelly to a ceiling.

Geoff's metaphor can sum it up sometimes – encouraging isn't it?

Your business plan will clarify your thoughts and help you to identify elements you need to consider – in short, help to set your jelly. Once you have been in business for a couple of months you can measure your figures against those you projected in your plan. This will allow you to adjust and spot any potential problems – and I hope avoid adding yourself to the failure statistics!

Though the other way you could look at it is to consider the plan your first sales document. Get other people to read it and give their views. You could also look on it as a job description for you. A job description is something we self-employed don't get the opportunity to have. Well now is your chance to write one. When you've written your plan, ask yourself if you're the person to be carrying this through. What training or help might you need to get going?

After all, a business plan is simply bringing together answers to the questions you have been asking yourself about your idea. 'Business plan' is just a fancy name for written-down common sense, really.

Business Plan Myths

There are some cracking myths about the production of a business plan.

'Size'

'My plan needs to be big to impress. The more pages, the better my chances of funding.'

Wrong – content is the key.

'Only About Finance'

A dazzling cash flow will look good by itself.

Wrong – the whole plan will need to answer those people who say 'prove it!' to you.

'Get Someone Else to Write It'

Yes, there are business plan writing services. They'll do the best job.

Wrong – you write it, this is your life. The first thing a contractor will add is a disclaimer.

'File It – Forget It'

Put it away and then forget all about it.

Wrong – review it and check your progress.

'Only for Large Businesses'

Large-style business plans are written by committee members who only work on their own section. They are often aimed at impressing investors and the writers don't really own the plan – if anything, a plan is more important to us.

'It's In My Head'

No need for a plan; no need to write it all down.

Wrong – well, if your head is getting anything like mine, the hard drive is getting overloaded.

Business Plan Contents

One of the most important elements to get in your first business plan is the 'WOW' factor. Business bank managers and grant-awarding people see loads of business plans, often produced by an accountant or some other third party – who incidentally will usually add a disclaimer to the plan. Avoid this negativity from the word 'go' by writing your own plan!

While a professionally-written plan will have all the right ingredients it won't have the 'WOW' factor – only you can provide that. So if you choose to employ a third party to write your plan, make sure you understand what they have produced for you and at least try to write the 'selling you' bits. After all, that's what your first plan is – a sales tool possibly to persuade a bank manager to part with his money. And even if you do not need funding to start, write a plan anyway because this document is going to be one of the most important things you ever write.

Forecast
The pretence of knowing what would have happened if what does happen hadn't.
Ralph Harris

A typical business plan will contain the following:

Objectives
What will this business do? What do you hope to achieve in the first year? What is your target by year two and three? Where do you want to be?

These need to be clear and simple aims – a bank manager will see through waffle. Make sure you set yourself objectives and keep reminding yourself just why you are doing this! A friend of mine was in business for one reason only – to retire to Morocco by the time he was 45. Did he do it? Yes, but it took until he was 47. His was an interesting case to study. He could detach himself from the business, no bother. At the end of the working day he would lock the doors, walk away and switch off. But as soon as he was back the next day, he would look at his calendar with views of Morocco and get all motivated again. The question is: what is your trigger? Lifestyle, I bet – it often is. There's nothing wrong with that. Though some business start-up organisations will scoff if you say so. But that's their problem.

Personal Background

Personnel Profile of all key people – and what skills they bring to the business.

This is where you can sell yourself. Point out what you are really good at and how that will be important to your business. At the same time check your SWOT analyses (Strengths, Weaknesses, Opportunities and Threats) and be honest with your Strengths and Weaknesses.

Compare them to the Opportunities you are looking at but bear in mind any Threats, such as legislation that might affect your business. Also, consider your health and check your health insurance. The bank manager will prompt you on this one. Be warned – one of the major contributors to business failure is 'poor health', so look after yourself!

Suppliers

Who are they and what trading terms do they offer you? This will influence your cash flow, for better or worse. If a supplier asks you for money up front (a pro forma invoice) then make sure you ask for a discount. After all, they are getting your money up front and if you don't ask you won't get.

The Market

Aha, the fun stuff. Some start-ups love market research. It can almost become an end in itself. I may choose to call it procrastination, but then I'm an old sceptic!

What research have you done? Who will be your typical customer? Have you done a SWOT analysis on your competitors? Is your business seasonal? Why will customers come to you rather than your competitors? How do you plan to promote your business?

Some hard questions here, often skipped by start-ups – DON'T skip them! We'll look at these topics in more detail later.

Financial Projections

What will your sales be each month/quarter/year? What will your gross profit be? Have you calculated your gross profit margin? What are your annual overheads? What is your break-even point? What is your estimated profit? Have you double-checked your survival income? (Come on, be honest – that's the important one, isn't it?) Does the cash-flow forecast tally? What will it cost to start and where is the funding coming from?

Again more on this riveting stuff later.

Seeing the Bank for Funding?

If you are seeing a bank manager to discuss your plan (for a loan or not), get your plan to him or her a few days before your meeting. This will give the bank manager a chance to read it in advance and to do your plan justice. You may have spent months producing this plan and the decision to lend or not might hinge on something missed if the plan is read in a hurry.

More on those bank creatures later.

Premises/Equipment

Itemise the equipment you need and the stuff you've already got. Where will you work from? If from home, will the rest of the family be a nuisance? Just as an aside, I work from home and some people including my wife, bless her, find it confusing. Why don't I 'go to work'?

Legal Issues

What form of business will you take – sole trader, partnership or limited company? Have you checked out health and safety? Can you use that stunning business name you've come up with? What insurance cover will you need? I'll never forget the start-up who was planning to do a book-keeping service and said that no insurance was needed. Oh yeah, think twice pal. How about indemnity insurance?

Key People
Not just you, but solicitors, accountants, advisers – all those who have helped you in a professional capacity. Name them.

So, there you have it: the bones of a business plan. How about an example? Well, the following plan was produced by a therapist and may help to explain the theory.

This plan was drawn up as part of a start-up programme I was involved with some years ago. The aim was for clients to produce a business plan which they could choose to present, or not, for a start-up grant. The format was geared around a series of questions. Clients could choose to keep their plan in that format or use it as a prompt to lay out in a style suited to their targeted funding source. Although basic, it served the purpose well – to question assumptions.

Financial projections and appendices to support the research, etc., were added. The gaps in the text are there to protect confidential information. I'm happy to add that the client is doing well and at the time of writing expanding her business in Herefordshire.

Incidentally, this client is female – and as a rough general-isation, it is my experience that they write better business plans than males!

Example Business Plan

OBJECTIVES
1. What will your business do?
Provide caring, sympathetic, high-quality complementary health care and personal effectiveness training through the disci-plines of _____ to the people of

'some county' within a 30-mile radius of
_____ and _____. Supplement
individual sessions with training opportunities organised with international and
local trainers. I will be working as a
sole trader from _____ Clinic,
and from home. I also hope eventually to
do some work in a hospice. I will trade
as a Sole Trader.

> Clear and simple objectives – no fancy waffle!
> Business bank managers will see through spin.

**2. What do you hope to achieve in the
first year of trading?**
a) I want to have established a customer
base of at least xx people in the first
year so I have a core of regular clients
coming for weekly health maintenance and
continuing personal development.
b) I want to see at least xx people a week
for sessions/treatments.
c) I want to have created a good local
(within 30-mile radius) reputation for
high-quality, caring and effective
bodywork/healing.
d) I want to have hosted my first training
course for international trainers and
therapists.
e) I want to at least be able to meet all
my personal expenses plus the business's
outlay. Ideally, I would like the business
to make a profit in the first year of
trading, but as a minimum to be meeting my
survival income. See appendix attached.

> Good – but could be a bit more bullish perhaps. I would prefer to use 'will have' instead of 'want to', though this is only a minor point.

3. How do you expect the business to be doing in three years?

Assuming 2 is achieved I would expect my customer base to have expanded to xx+ in three years' time. I expect client referrals to be working well by this time and for the network of people using my service and aware of my reputation to be steadily increasing. I would expect to be seeing xx – xx people a week for sessions/treatment. I aim to be increasing the business's profit in order that I can start saving to buy my own property (home with session space) and set up a really special environment for clients to relax in during and after their session/treatment. The property would include a meditation garden and relaxation room. I would expect to be running at least two seminars a year for my increasing training client group and other interested individuals.

4. Give brief details of your personal and business background: vocational and academic qualifications.

I am a skilled body worker with just under 10 years' experience of client work (previously with part-time employment in associated fields). I work in a respectful, heart- and person-centred way with an emphasis on the client as the expert on him or herself. I have helped clients in gaining freedom from long-term physical conditions, in tackling long-standing life issues and in moving forward in positive new ways in their lives. I have a passionate enthusiasm for this work and the potential it can unlock in individuals.

> Remember: Always add evidence to back up your plan and skills, as appendices.

My business will rely on my personal qualities as well as my technical competence. As part of this, an emphasis must be my own self-nurturing and health. It will be important to teach by example as much as possible — a healer who knows how to look after herself will be able to encourage others to do likewise. I am committed to this work and what it can offer clients and me in terms of personal satisfaction.

I have also worked for 4 years as a part-time administrator for The _____ Association and have developed the good organisational and administrative skills essential to a successful business. I have now also supplemented this with business training provided by the xxxxxx xxxxxxx xxxxxx Programme.

For development, I see the need to promote myself more to my target client groups. Over the last 5 or 6 years I have developed the skills to talk to local groups about what I do and how it can benefit them. I will need to do this more as I feel this will prove the best form of advertising.

5. What would happen to your business if you fall ill or injured?

In the event of temporary illness or injury, I have a 'bank' of 2 practitioners who could cover my client sessions so I do not lose clients through absence. For long-term or permanent illness/injury, my partner and family would finance me and I have a Disabling Injuries insurance policy in case of injury.

Good – don't forget to get health insurance cover.

---

6. Give details of other Partners or Co-Directors who will be involved in the business.

None.

YOUR SUPPLIERS
7. Who will be your major supplier(s)? What are their terms and conditions of business?

I need little stock for running my business. My main tools are my hands. I will buy massage oil, antiseptic wipes and plasters, and flowers and candles to enhance the treatment room environment, purchased from retail outlets.

Add suppliers' details, terms, etc., to the appendices. Wonderful thing these extras!

YOUR MARKET

8. What research have you done to find out the need for your product or service?

a) Researched competitors. There are no other _____ practitioners within a 12 mile radius and only one other in the county. There is 1 _____ practitioner 4 miles away aiming at a different market (those using her retreat/B&B space). Other than that all other _____ practitioners are working 10 or more miles away. There is one aromatherapist and one reflexologist within my immediate area, the former operates on a spare-time basis from home and the latter works from a hairdresser's, aiming more at that market, again on a part-time basis.

I also collected information on 30 complementary health practitioners advertising within a 10-12 mile radius of _____. 3 were medical herbalists, 2 were homoeopaths and 1 a colour therapist - so they are not direct competitors as they are not offering a form of bodywork. 9 practised some counselling or psychotherapy — again not disciplines which work through bodywork. Their work stresses the psyche and does not directly address body issues, although obviously work on one affects the other. I feel both groups will attract a different customer group.

15 practised some form of bodywork. There were 3 _____ practitioners, 7 were masseurs/aromatherapists and reflexologists, 1 a shiatsu practitioner, 1 an

Alexander teacher and 2 were cranio-sacral practitioners.
1 practised _____ but is a close colleague of mine and her main work is outside my area in _____

> Very thorough – remember competition is good, it proves a need.

While it is difficult to assess the strengths and weaknesses of the body workers without taking sessions from all of them, I did notice from their publicity information that only one person stood out from the rest. Her information was clear, concise and she highlighted her experience. She managed to suggest a certain confidence. Much of the advertising was poorly and cheaply produced and there was little to distinguish between them. I noticed that I was more drawn to advertising that introduced the therapist as well as the therapy. It highlighted the need to design my own advertising to take in these points and distinguish myself from the crowd.

All 30 practitioners practise at least 10 miles away from my home clinic, one being as far away as _____. All but 4 practise 20 miles away from the clinic I use in _____.

b) Surveyed 15 colleagues on my _____ course to discover reaction to my literature and their likelihood of using my service. 4 responded, 3 positively, one of whom is going to book a session and another who did book a session with me.

> Great – tested the promotional material and got some feedback.

c) Recently talked to 20 people at the local pensioners' group, clearly identified the need for complementary care for health problems, major and minor, and a willingness to try healing. 40% had a trial session and gave favourable comments including the desire to come for treatment.

9. What opportunities and threats is the market presenting?

Opportunities:
Complementary therapy is a growing market as the public becomes more aware of the potential benefits of this kind of health care. I find that more and more people are becoming aware of complementary therapy and more people want to move away from medication with health-compromising 'side effects'. In XXXX alone, there were at least 3 articles on _____ in the national press (for example: *Daily Express*, *The Guardian*, *The Times*, *Daily Mail*, *Harpers' Bazaar*, *SHE*, *Woman & Home*, *Positive Health*, *InterAction for M.E.*, *Here's Health*, *Women's Health*).

_____ is becoming a household name in the same way as acupuncture and aromatherapy have done.

> I repeat again – include copies of articles in the appendices.

As the pace of life increases, more and more people are searching for ways to reduce stress, create relaxation and sacred space in an often time-pressured and demanding lifestyle. Fewer people are now willing to resort to tranquillisers, sleeping tablets and the like to combat stress. People are seeking more life-enhancing alternatives. People want to find slots in their week in which to include relaxation, exercise and therapy. This offers huge potential for my work and the service I offer, often providing a haven 'to put back in, what life takes out'. I aim to develop towards providing an extended period of relaxation for clients using my service. For example, after a session clients may wish to relax in a specially created environment indoors or outdoors to maximise the benefit from their session/treatment.

> Good stuff – preparing the sales pitch!

Also, the NHS is increasingly taking complementary therapy more seriously. I contacted an ex-colleague at _____ Healthcare NHS Trust about the Integrated Complementary Health Policy they are about to implement. They are recognising the valid role of complementary therapy in patient care and this can only lead to an increase in opportunities for practitioners in the future. _____ is a forward-thinking health trust, and my experience of working there for 5 years showed that other trusts were often keen to follow once the groundwork had been done. I am also interested in working in a hospice environment with terminally ill cancer patients. I am making some connections by means of a cancer patient I am currently treating. There is also a Parliamentary Early Day Motion calling for cancer patients to be able to choose complementary therapy over chemotherapy and other conventional cancer treatment if they wish to do so and have this funded by the NHS. This could potentially lead to legislation and would widen the opportunities for complementary therapists working with groups who might not be able to finance their own treatment.

> Excellent – back up from a powerful third party.

My rural location means that rural dwellers do not have to travel to _____ for sessions/treatment. I am in the heart of their local community. However, if those living further afield want to come to my practice, I am easily reached by car or the local bus service.

Threats:
More people are training in complementary therapy each year. However, many of these are via local technical colleges and are focused on the beauty end of the market. They are obviously also not experienced yet in the field, and many will be under

20 and therefore not bringing life experience to their work. I have just under 10 years' experience as a part-time practitioner working for others, and I bring my own self-healing experiences to my practice.

People in the UK are not used to paying directly for their health care. Health care is considered to be 'free' through the NHS. However, I feel that this view is changing and have been surprised recently that, for example, pensioners are willing to pay my full fee (£xx) without any request for concessions. The younger generation is now growing up with the notion of paying for complementary care with other services such as private pensions, etc.

There are some bodywork practitioners already working in my immediate area. However, they all appear to be low-profile and many only run as a part-time concern. It feels to me that there is plenty of room for my service especially as what I'm offering includes _____ which is new to the area and includes personal effectiveness training (getting people to take a holistic look at their lives and what they want to achieve and create in them) rather than only focusing on physical therapy.

Understand what makes your competition tick.

10. Who will be your typical customer?

The people I'm hoping to have as clients fall into 4 distinct (but not necessarily mutually exclusive) categories:

People within a 30 mile radius of
_____

a) Seeking help with physical ailments, emotional/behavioural challenges, stress and tension.

b) Wishing to achieve personal potential and empowerment by addressing all the experiences, past and present, which compromise future possibilities.

c) Wishing to receive healing as part of their transition through death (hospice work).

d) Seeking to further (b) by taking up training opportunities organised through me.

Tricky question this. I remember one drain-clearing business start-up put 'Everybody needs me, because everybody has got a toilet.' How did he do? Went down those drains he wanted to unblock, I'm afraid to say.

---

11. Is your business or market seasonal? If seasonal, what will you do in the 'off' season?

My business is seasonal as I expect less work in the summer months (people feel better and more positive when there is more light) especially August when many people go on holiday. Also, pre- and post-Christmas people spend less on what they might consider a 'luxury'. During these periods I will take my own holidays and also use the time to redesign my advertising literature to keep the information fresh and updated.

> Every business is seasonal with peaks and troughs. You can holiday in your troughs!

12. What will your customers want or expect from you and why will they need what you offer?

Clients will want some or all of the following:

- A solution to health problems — physical, mental and emotional.
- An enjoyable vehicle for achieving personal potential and empowerment by addressing all the experiences, past and present, which compromise future possibilities. To receive healing as part of their transition to death (hospice work).
- To be offered access to training opportunities to strengthen work done in individual sessions/treatments.

They will need what I am offering because of the following benefits:

- Freedom from physical, emotional and mental pain.
- Alleviation of stress and tension.
- Achievement of greater personal satisfaction/success in work and other aspects of their lives.
- Ability to learn to operate from a place of choice rather than obligation.

> In other words – what's in it for the customer. How can they benefit?

13. How will you promote your product or service? How much will it cost to promote and sell?

My main form of advertising will be talks, demonstrations and a series of open-days offering short taster sessions. The cost for these will be small. I will also produce business cards and a comprehensive brochure outlining the features and benefits of my service. I will spend time each week ensuring that relevant places have stocks of these leaflets (that is, local healthfood shops, cafés and other shops with noticeboard space). I will run a monthly advert in _____ for 12 months and may try a magazine called _____ which gets exposure in supermarkets.

Advertising Costs:
Business cards (200)   £
Brochures (1,000)   £
Advertisements   £
TOTAL   £

14. Who will your competitors be? What are their strengths and weaknesses?
See 8 and 9 above and appendices.

15. Why will your customers prefer you to your competitors?
Clients will prefer me to my competitors because of the confidence they can have in my ten years of experience as a body worker. I look beyond the symptoms to the

root cause of disease. Once they understand the root, the solution is in their
own hands not those of the 'experts'. I
offer people's lives and well-being into
their own keeping. This is incredibly
empowering.

PREMISES, EQUIPMENT & VEHICLES
**16. List the premises, equipment and
vehicles you will need for your business.**
[Indicate the estimated cost of those
items to be bought.]

Car	£
Treatment couch	£
Treatment couch linen	£
Blankets	£
Paint walls: treatment room	£
Rug	£
Mobile chair or stool	£
Room hire (clinic)	£
TOTAL	£

MONEY
**17. How much will it cost to set up your
business?**
£ xxxx

Remember: start-up usually costs more than you
expect. And takes longer!

---

18. Where will you get the money to start your business?
Applying for a discretionary grant or putting in own money from private account overdraft facility.

See Financial Projections attached.

PROFESSIONAL/LEGAL ISSUES AND ADVICE
19. Have you had any professional advice about your business proposal?
The _____ Association has provided me with information about legal issues - see attached. Also consulted the following:
_____ Training Programme
XXX Bank business pack
Advertising Consultant
Accountant
Solicitor.

> Don't be afraid to speak to as many people as you can.

And just to finish on...
Overleaf is an irreverent (or is it cynical?) look at business plan terminology and their true definitions – it is just for fun!

Business Plan Term	Real Meaning
'is proven technology'	'well, it almost worked once'
'unique'	'apart from the other twelve competitors'
'cash-flow problem'	'about to go bust'
'complex system'	'nobody understands it'
'core business'	'our only activity'
'clear projections'	'blink and you'll miss them'
'performance analysis'	'OK, heads or tails?'
'niche market'	'only one customer'
'protective approach'	'ready and willing to copy'
'revised budget'	'getting closer to the truth'

3

THE MONEY BIT

Right, hold that yawn, this bit will be exciting. Though I did once send a client to sleep when covering this topic on a start-up course. The strange thing is, he came up at the end and said how much he had enjoyed the session!

Be honest now – this is the chapter you were hoping would be last, or that you could flick through. Don't worry, I am in the same league – but after helping many start-ups and seeing the look of panic in their eyes at the mere mention of a cash flow, remember, you are not alone.

This part will be basic and I hope provide a starting point which you could take deeper, if you want, with an accountant. The big problem is that far too many financial types have, in the past, made the topic too dry. Or, worse, kept it shrouded in mystery like it was some strange black art not fit for us mere mortals. Well, I'm glad to say things have improved and I do know some accountants who are both human and down-to-earth. See? I don't have a go at everyone.

> **Finance**
> The art of passing currency from hand to hand until it finally disappears.
> *Robert W Sarnoff*

Now I know what you are like – you just want to get on and start and run your business. 'I'll worry about the money stuff later,' I hear you say. Listen, pal: I don't have a finance background but, take it from me, it is important. Yes, I know all the fancy jargon sends you dizzy. But look on it like this; it is merely budgeting and managing money and every time you go off down to the pub you do this. How much money have I got? How many drinks can I have? But hang on I can't spend it all because I need to pay the phone bill... you get the idea. There you go: budgeting. And please don't be one of the 'I'm far too creative, I'm not good with figures.' That is a common phrase from the craft business start-ups, and, to be honest from some non-craft type businesses as well. If it is true, then get trained; at least try to follow the rudiments of the money stuff. That way if you employ a book-keeper or accountant you have some idea what they are talking about and your eyes won't glaze over as much.

Do you need a book-keeper or accountant? This is a frequent question from start-ups. It depends how complicated your finances are going to be. There is a strong argument for having help. This would then allow you time to get on and do what you are best at – making and selling your product or service. And, of course, there is the fact that most good accountants will get their fee from the tax they may well save you from paying. As an aside (and you may not like this) in business it is a good indicator if you are paying tax. 'Good grief, the man has taken leave of his senses!' you scream. Well, no – not completely. To pay tax you need to be making a profit – and why are we in business? What you want from your accountant is to minimize your tax liability so you have more funds to invest in the business.

Credit
A system of buying time with money you don't have.
Joey Adams

Survival Income

So let's have a look at the jargon stuff and how it relates to you. The first bit to get to grips with is your survival income requirement. In other words, what you need every month to do simply that – survive.

When I hear start-ups or small businesses say they don't know how to set their sales target, I point out that they can, by starting at their survival income. After all, you need to know the minimum you need to survive.

Be warned; it is always more than you imagine when you're calculating the figures. A good idea is to add a 10 per cent contingency to your final figure. This will cover those bits you may have forgotten and Murphy's Law.

Survival Income

Mortgage/Rent	....
Council Tax/Water Rates	....
Gas, electricity and oil	....
All personal and property insurance	....
Food, general housekeeping expenses	....
Clothing	....
Telephone	....
Hire charges (TV, DVD, etc.)	....
Entertainment (meals and drink)	....
Subscriptions to associations, journals, etc.	....
Car Tax and insurance	....
Car: running expenses	....
Car: service and maintenance	....
Children's expenditure and presents	....
Savings plans	....
HP/Credit Card repayments	....
Holiday/Christmas	....
Other (list)	....
Sub Total	....
Plus Contingencies 10%	....
Total: EXPENDITURE (a)	_____

ESTIMATED INCOME	....
Income from family/partner (total)	....
Other income (state)	....
Total: INCOME* (see overleaf) **(b)**	_____

Total: SURVIVAL INCOME	_____
required in the year i.e. (a) less (b)	

*if your estimated expenditure (a) exceeds your estimated income (b) then you need to calculate how much money you need to invest in your business.

If your Survival Income is negative – there is spare cash. Whoopee!

How does this help when you have just been off to the bank and asked for a loan to fund your business idea? Well, you have started to calculate what your business needs to bring in for you to survive – not a bad starting point. However, more than likely they will have turned around to you and asked for a cash flow and profit and loss projections. They may not. You might only need to have flashed a letterhead and give an appreciating nod to get your hands-on the spondoolies. I have seen it happen. But you can be sure the bank felt they had security and that their money was safe.

Incidentally, an obliging bank manager told me the criteria they apply when looking at borrowing. In simple terms, they want to see, after all the business bills and wages/drawings have been paid, that the balance of profit remaining is three times the annual repayments to the bank. Now look – don't go away and manipulate those figures to comply with this principle!

Have they asked you for a cash flow and a profit and loss forecast? Or maybe asked if you know what your break-even figure has to be? Hey, you may even be curious to know this information as well. In fact, don't just be curious: let's get serious for a moment – you need to know this stuff! You may have been given some strange-looking forms to complete to produce the cash flow and profit and loss. And don't you know it, they look sort of similar. A bit like the old battleship game you used to play, perhaps. The first thing to appreciate is that you need not complete every single box. Some parts may not apply to your business. Although they look similar in layout there are some subtle differences.

In simple terms, the cash flow is only concerned with how you plan to budget the everyday movement of cash in and out of your business, while the profit and loss shows the increase (or loss!) of profit within the business. It will take a broader look at the business, start at zero balance and will identify whether you will make enough profit to pay yourself. A good definition is that it shows how effectively you buy and sell, in other words, how effectively you can trade.

Your cash flow will show your personal drawings and any initial cash placed into the business. It will also show when you hope to get paid. After all, if you issue an invoice in June you know that it could take two to three months before you may actually get your hands on it!

Which is more important, cash flow or profit and loss? Oh, how I wish you hadn't asked that question. Me, well I like cash but they are both important as gauges to how your business is doing. Don't bury your head in the sand – you need to know this stuff. And while we are on it, don't confuse cash in your pocket with profit. A much wiser finance head than I explained the difference between cash and profit very simply. Slowly he said to me, 'If you buy stock at £1 and sell it for £2 – easy, your profit is £1. What if you buy double the amount of stock? So you have spent £2 but if you only sell half of it – well, your profit is still £1 – but have you got any cash left?'

Business Costs

Now this is all very well, but we should pause for a moment to see how your business costs work. Business costs generally get split into two camps. Those that are fixed no matter how much business you do and those that are variable on the business you do. In other words, the fixed ones are the nasty ones. For example, if you have a shop they include rent, rates, insurance and utilities; if you employ anybody you have to factor in their wages. Irrespective of how much business you do, you will be paying these every month. That's why they are called 'fixed', though you may also see them referred to as indirect costs or overheads. Whatever title they go under, they are a pain and you want to keep a close eye on them. Any opportunity you get to reduce them, seize!

The effect of discounting

Another simple calculation!

Sell at	10
Buy at	7
Gross Profit	3
Overheads	2.50
Net Profit	0.50

What if we give a 10% discount?

Sell at	9
Buy at	7
Gross Profit	2
Overheads	2.50
Net Profit	−0.50

What if we put our price up by 10%?

Sell at	11
Buy at	7
Gross Profit	4
Overheads	2.50
Net Profit	1.50

Now, I know this is Janet and John maths, but it shows the impact of discounting without giving it due care and thought.

Your variable costs will fluctuate in line with the business you win. They include materials and casual staff that you bring in to cover busy periods. Another name they go under is direct costs. That one is easy to remember, because they are directly related to your sales.

Achievement
Behind every achievement is a proud wife and a surprised mother-in-law.
Brooks Hays

So how do these figures fit into the overall picture of your business? Well, they will help you to compile a profit and loss statement or forecast. They will influence your gross profit margin and, of course, your profit or loss. 'But what about little old me and my wages?' you cry. Well, from now on get used to referring to your wages as 'drawings'. Why? The taxman looks on your wages as 'drawings' against the profit of your business. And let's knock this one on the head right now – you are taxed on your profit; in other words, the source of your drawings . . .One start-up was convinced that HMRC did not tax his drawings. Oh, how I wish this was true. I would start paying myself all my profit to avoid tax. Get it clear now – I'll say it again, paying tax in business is a good thing. No I haven't lost the plot; it means you are making a profit. What a good accountant will do is minimize the amount payable so you can invest and expand your business. Your accountant will help you avoid some tax – if he ever talks about evading tax, sack him!

Profit
Whatever you make in business – if you don't make a profit, you won't make it for long.
Anon

If we look at gross profit, gross profit margin and net profit next we can then put together an example profit and loss projection and you can see where these darn things fit together.

Overhead Number 1
Overhead number 1 is YOU.
Don't forget why you are in business – to pay yourself.

Some financial types will tell you to include your survival income requirement in your overheads total.

If you choose to put yourself at the end coming out of the profit figure it doesn't matter – just as long as there is more than enough to meet your survival income.

Paying yourself – and regularly – is one of the many **'landmark'** points in the growth of you and your business.

Still with me? OK, here we go. What is the difference between gross and net profit? And how do I work out my gross profit margin? Why is it important for me to know them? Your mates currently in business have got by without thinking about them. Well good luck to them – you look after your business and leave them to blunder through theirs! You need to have some idea how your business is performing and every business has a rule of thumb for what these figures should be. An accountant will know them as does the taxman. And don't you want to know how you compare?

By Way of Explanation
In very basic terms:

Gross Profit
Indicates how well you buy and sell, and you want to do both of those well.

Net Profit
Indicates how well you run your business.

> It would be folly to buy and sell badly but run your business efficiently. You want to do it all properly.

Now, there is a wonderful short-cut to get to the gross profit, gross profit margin, break even and net profit. It goes under the unlikely name of the Genghis Khan Financial Projections. Don't ask me why. All I know is that when it was shown to me for the first time I was speechless at how simple it is. And making me speechless takes some doing!

The Genghis Khan Financial Projections
This straightforward system is based on work carried out by an academic. I would dearly like to give credit to the originator, but I think he or she may have been lost in the mists of time. Don't panic – it is not academic mumbo-jumbo but a practical way of calculating your gross profit, gross profit margin, break-even and estimated profit (or loss!). Here we go.

Step One is to calculate your sales or predicted sales if you are a start-up.

Step Two is to total up your cost of materials to produce your product and the cost of any sub-contractors – the variable/direct costs. Not your drawings or staff wages. Now take them away from your sales figure and you have your gross profit figure.

Step Three requires you to divide your sales figure into your gross profit, multiply by 100 and then you have your gross profit margin, expressed as a percentage.
    Still with us?

Step Four is to total up your overheads – fixed/indirect costs – again either predicted or from your records.

Step Five is to divide your overheads total by your gross profit margin figure. Multiply by 100 and, lo and behold, you have your annual sales turnover required to break even. Your business will 'break-even' when your gross profit is equal to the fixed costs of the business. If your sales fall below this figure you are making a loss. Above the figure you are making a profit. You could divide it by 12 to get a monthly figure if you want; and divide by 4 to get a weekly figure. I suppose you could calculate it down to the hour if you wanted to! Anyway back to the plot.

Step Six is to take your annual break-even sales figure from your sales total from Step One. Multiply it by your gross profit margin from Step Three and you will have a figure that shows your estimated or actual profit.

But to help how about an example? So, as the saying goes – here is one I did earlier.

Step One:
Projected Annual Sales   **23,600**

Step Two:
Materials	7,000
Labour Costs	0
Total Direct Costs	7,000
GROSS PROFIT	**16,600**

Step Three: GROSS PROFIT MARGIN   **70%**
(Divide 16,600 by 23,600; multiply answer by 100)

Step Four:
Calculate your **OVERHEADS** for the year   **9,350**

Step Five:
Divide 9,350 by 70 multiply by 100
To give **ANNUAL BREAK-EVEN FIGURE**   **13,357**
(Divide by 12 for monthly (1,113))

Step Six:
23,600 minus 13,357 multiplied by 70
divided by 100
ESTIMATED PROFIT 7,170

OK, now what do you do with these figures you've worked out?

Simple: lay them out as a summary sheet in the financial section of your   business plan. So our example would look like this:

Financial Summary for My Wonderful Business
Projected Sales:	23,600
Direct Costs:	7,000
Gross Profit:	16,600
Gross Profit Margin:	70%
Overheads:	9,350
Break Even:	13,357
Estimated Profit:	7,170

Isn't that neater than graphs and charts? OK maybe include them as appendices by way of an explanation for the figures. Your typical business bank manager is going to hug you with relief.

Well, almost. Because there is always a catch isn't there? Some of you may have already spotted it. What about your drawings? Where are they in the calculations? That's right, you can't see them. So where do they come from? Easy – from the profit. So are you going to make enough profit to pay yourself? If not, then why are you doing this? When will the profit become enough?

Right, that's enough of the jargon. Back to making money.

How Can You Arrive at a Sales Target When You Are a New Business?
As a simple way of setting a sales target you could try the following. But be warned, some business advisers are not going to approve of this approach. Too simplistic for their liking, I expect.

When talking to your local business bank manager (how a bank manager thinks)

Never say:
'I have the greatest idea since sliced bread – and nobody else is doing it.'

Bank managers are by nature not risk takers. You are not talking to a venture capitalist. They went into banking as a secure career option and in you trot asking for money against an idea that they will perceive as a risk. Phrases like 'no one else is doing this in this town' or 'it is completely unique' will get them reaching for oxygen.
   Stress that your idea is as old as time – but you have a new twist on it.

Suppose your survival income comes to £1,000 per month. Add your business expenses, which for this example now takes it to £1,250 a month. Add 15 per cent as a contingency and for convenience we will round the total up to £1,440. No matter how optimistic you are, you will not work every day of the year – and you don't want to either!

So how about estimating that you actually 'earn' for three days a week?

Spread over a 48-week year (48 because you want a holiday some time) will give 144 earning days in the year. In other words 12 a month. Yes, I know we could have arrived at this figure sooner!

Therefore £1,440 divided by 12 equals £120 per 'earning' day. So, if you do £150 on an 'earning' day you toddle off home, or to the pub, happy and content. Get the drift? But what about a business that needs to buy materials? You could quote your clients a rate plus materials; with your materials marked up a rate to cover your sourcing of the materials. I have known several gardeners start off by simply charging for their time/labour and using plants/materials supplied by their clients.

Farmyard story

I recall a start-up who made wonderful, old-fashioned, wooden farmyards.

When he said how much he sold them for I was certain he was undervaluing his product.

When asked how he had arrived at his price, he responded, 'from my costs'.

'What about your time?' I asked.

'Oh, I don't add that,' he explained. 'I'm doing it anyway.'

'What about the market price?' I queried.

'The what?' came his reply.

OK, to cut a long story short. After some market research, he could triple his price and still be competitive. He duly put up his prices. I am not recommending ripping off your customers but you must get what you are worth!

Which sort of leads to this . . .

Hourly Rate

Do you like to be charged by the hour? I bet your answer is 'No'. You prefer a price for the job. OK, then you ask, 'How long will it take?' You may do some mental arithmetic, but I doubt it. If the price sounds about right, you are happy.

So why not apply this idea to your business? It will make you stand out from the crowd.

Now this is all very well but when you come to charging out your hourly rate your research needs to find out what the 'going rate' is in your expertise and the local area. That £120 per day could equate to just over £15 per hour, at an eight-hour day. Well, we all know what skilled plumbers will charge per hour and it is more than that £15 an hour! Know your market and know what you are worth to it.

Don't fall into the 'I can be cheaper and will pick up more work' trap. Why rock the market rate? Generally, clients are happy to pay the going rate and if you pitch it too cheap you make them suspicious. 'Must be something wrong with it,' they say. I am not advocating 'Rip off Britain'. Just make sure you get what your expertise, knowledge and time are worth.

Funding Sources

But how does all this help you to raise money to start your business? Are these projections just to impress the bank so they can tick their boxes? Well, call me an old cynic, but if you ask me to lend you some money I want to know that I will get it back. Your forecasts will demonstrate you know what you are doing and may help sway the funding decision in your favour. And please don't forget to keep doing these calculations or work with your accountant on them. You will find them so much easier to do when you have actual figures to work with!

Where are your possible sources of funding? Funding that your calculations have shown that you need. See, we are getting all cocky about them now, aren't we!

This has to be one of the most frequent questions! Where can I get funding or a grant to help me start my business?

High Street Banks

High street banks are the largest providers of start-up funding. Up to 75 per cent of start-ups use bank loans to raise start-up funds and as a general rule they like you to match their investment pound for pound! The remainder usually comes from savings, redundancy, or friends and relatives. Sometimes your local authority will offer a small discretionary start-up grant and you should contact your local council's business development section. As part of the eligibility you will probably be expected to undertake a short business start-up course and submit a business plan for approval – all stuff I would heartily endorse!

Looking for a grant?
Contact your local Enterprise Agency which has staff to help you through the grants maze!

A good business plan is vital when seeking any financial help. Again, use the services of local business support agencies – NEVER be too proud to ask for help, which is what they are there for!

Oh, and never pay a fee to anybody who claims he can source grants for you; it is not necessary.

Credit Cards
Please try to avoid using credit cards as a source of start-up funding. They are expensive sources of borrowing!

Local Authority
Your local authority may also offer some incentives on premises or work space as an encouragement to starting in their area. The UK is split into regions of differing support levels from the EU and this often dictates the amount of local authority support and funding available in your area.

Prince's Trust
If you are between 18 and 30, unemployed and don't have the means to start your business, then it could be worth contacting your local branch of the Prince's Trust.

Ex-Forces
If you are ex-forces, then make contact with start-up support and funds available from the British Legion – check with your local branch.

Business Link
Some grants are available from the Government. Find out the latest information by checking their websites: Business Link in England, Business Gateway in Scotland, Business Wales in Wales, and NI Business in Northern Ireland.

> **Government Grants**
> A system of making money taken from the people that look like a gift when handed back.
> *Carl Workman*

Job Centres

If you are unemployed check with your local Job Centre Plus about Enterprise Clubs and the New Enterprise Allowance. You could get help and financial support to set up your own business.

Venture Capital

Venture capital finances a start-up or growing business when a portion of the share capital or equity is sold in return for a major investment in the business. Some of your personal control over the business is lost to the new shareholder, but in return the investment can be substantial and get your business on a fast track – if that's what you want! Venture capitalists will invest sums over £250,000 while 'Business Angels' will look at lower figures. The British Private Equity and Venture Capital Association publishes a list of Venture Capital Funds.

Enterprise Finance Guarantee

The Enterprise Finance Guarantee (EFG) facilitates additional bank lending to small businesses which lack the security to secure a normal commercial loan. The Government provides the lender with a guarantee for which the borrower pays a premium. The lender administers the Enterprise Finance Guarantee and makes all the decisions on the lending.

For contact details for the above organisations, see the Appendix.

Big versus Small
What we are trying relentlessly to do is get that small company soul and speed inside our big company body.
Jack Welch

4

RESEARCH

Let me set the scene for you. There you are in the pub or bar with your friends. With the sort of warm glow that comes from having several drinks, you start to tell them about your great and unique business idea. They nod approvingly and agree that it will make you a fortune. After all, nobody else is doing it. Now, it may just stay at that stage or you may decide to jump in and start up in business. But how about asking yourself some questions? Or, better still, get someone else to be devil's advocate and ask you some questions. Questions that will need honest answers.

You may not like the questions but it is far better to get them over before you rush into something only to make a fool of yourself. After all, you want to avoid that nasty question: 'Why did it fail?' At this point it is worth stressing that successful businesses keep asking questions and never assume they know it all.

Sadly, far too many start-up and established businesses fail to grasp how important market research is to their survival. Consider the following sobering facts: only 40 per cent of start-ups make it into their third year and each week over 800 so-called 'established' businesses fail. That may encourage you to take market research a bit more seriously. While there will be many reasons behind these horrendous figures, poor or non-existent market research will be a strong contributory cause.

> **Market Research**
> What you call it when you already know the answer, but still hunt up the question that will produce it.
> *Robert Fuoss*

Often, start-ups will consider market research relevant only to the big boys.

Wrong!

Often they rely on their mates in the pub, taking comments like 'Yeah, that's a good idea, you don't see many of them about,' as being good enough research. After all, there may be a good reason you don't see many of them about! Take your friends' comments as a starting point and then get out there and check what the rest of the world has to say.

> **Think Laterally**
> *Try to prove that your idea is wrong.*
> Don't just listen to mates who say it is a wonderful idea. Seek out doubters and come up with answers to their negative questions and comments.
> Ask yourself why wouldn't they buy from me?
> In other words, come at your research from a different angle. Don't ever accept your assumptions are correct!

So, what do you want from your market research? Well, firstly you want to avoid adding to those frightening figures already mentioned, don't you? But you want answers to questions and you want information. Occasionally I am tempted to refer to the enthusiastic start-ups as 'information junkies'. This is a far more healthy approach than blundering along in business. Established businesses that succeed will keep this thirst for information, recognising that it will keep them ahead of their competitors and thus help them to stay in business. Your market research may just help reinforce what you already know and give your gut feeling some substance.

Any potential routes of funding, such as banks or sources of grants, will expect to see market research carried out. They, and you for that matter, shouldn't accept your proposal on face value and will keep saying 'prove it, prove it'. Remember financiers will see plenty of proposals, and they are unlikely to share your enthusiasm, being by nature a fairly sceptical bunch. Be prepared to answer some tough questions.

Questions to Ask
What products/service do your clients need?
Never assume that you know what they want. Keep finding out just what it is they require. Don't ever be a business with this attitude: 'You will buy what I want to sell.' Your awakening will be hard and cruel.

Where is the market?
Is it local, regional, national, or international? I recall one fledgling drains unblocker who dismissed the research stage with this comment: 'Everybody needs me, because everybody has a toilet.' Right, so how will you unblock a loo that's 300 miles away in Glasgow?

What is the market size – potential/target?
Avoid the 'everybody needs what I am offering' syndrome. To put it bluntly – they don't. It is back to the approach from our character in the last bit. How did his business do? Sad to say, the drain it disappeared down wasn't blocked at all.

What outside factors affect your market?
Legislation, local or national, may be presenting an opportunity or could be posing a threat. The owner of a mobile catering business with a static site in a town centre had to get an amendment to his licence so he could sell strawberries and cream during Wimbledon fortnight.

Who are your customers?
Draw up a profile or profiles of your potential customers. Remember not everybody wants your product or service.

Understand what makes your customers tick. What is important to them? Remember that something you think is trivial could be the clincher for your customers.

How will your customers' needs be satisfied?
Simple logistics of delivery or how they can get to you; make it too difficult for them and they will give up and go elsewhere. I will leave it up to the psychologists to cover the client's inner needs!

Who are your competitors?
Everybody has competition – never forget your customers have a choice. It may not be direct competition but other businesses that are trying to tempt your clients into opening their wallets. Remember competition is good. It proves the market. Praise them, say they are busy – it backs up the viability of your idea. And, if you can twist my arm and convince me that there is no competition, I will get all sanctimonious and say maybe there is no market either!

What is special about you?
Given that they have a choice – why choose you? And don't just say you are cheaper! Why should I come to you? Hint – do you offer good old-fashioned customer service?

What is your pricing structure?
Will you discount and why will you discount? Refer to the example in Chapter 7, *Running the Business,* and be sure you have your discounting fully covered.

How will you promote to your target customers?
What do they read and how can you stand out from the crowd? More later.

How much finance is needed?
Where is the funding going to come from and are there any grants available? All the above will cost you money. How I laughed and then cried when one start-up put in his plan that

he proposed to spend 'up to £50 a year promoting the business'. Wow, big spender, eh? That's right – less than £1 a week. He added that 'word of mouth' would be enough. More on that expression later!

Strewth, what a list, it's enough to make you reach for a very stiff drink! How and where are you going to find the answers to these questions? Fear not, there is a mountain of information about to satisfy your needs, and give the 'information junkie' a fix. At the end, there is an example of market research in action and a tip on how to get your research done.

Basically it boils down to two simple research processes, which are often referred to as 'desk' and 'field' research. Desk work will involve sitting behind a desk and fieldwork consists of out there and finding out about the world.

Sources of Market Research
So, which desks do you need to be pulling a chair up to, in order to carry out your market research? Be careful, because there can be a mountain of information waiting for you to climb, so have a deep intake of oxygen and avoid the avalanches ahead – poor pun, but be ready for an overload!

Banks
Local bank managers can be good sources of information, because they know what is going on in your area. If your business is regional, national, or global try to speak to someone higher up in their organisation.

For example, high street bank managers will have good local knowledge and contacts you may find very useful. Some banks may offer a 'Grant Search' for a fee. This could save you much leg work with tracking down grants – of which there are apparently nearly 3,000 available, from various sources!

Libraries
The reference section of your local library will have various useful publications to help you with your research. Check out these:

The UK Media Directory or BRAD – British Readership and Data. Most magazines, newspapers and trade journals published in this country are listed in this large directory. Find those that are relevant to your business and ask for a sample copy – say that you are considering advertising. Get them and you will be able to source plenty of relevant information about your sector and competition. Often trade magazines will reproduce surveys and reports from market research organisations.

Key Note Reports – these are expensive and libraries don't allow photocopying! However, they will give information and analyses of particular business areas, with emphasis on trends and future developments. Extract the information and include it as a source in your final research report.

Your local library may carry the handy little *NTC Pocket Books*. These are heaving with statistics about employment, education, finance, shopping, leisure and loads of other topics. They are useful in showing trends and consumer patterns. Although this information can be a bit too general, you should get information that will help to answer the question about the market expanding or shrinking.

If you get a good reference librarian on your side, he or she will trawl out a mountain of useful directories to help you with your research. One of the best sources of business information is Business Insight at Birmingham's Central Library (see the Appendix), and if you cannot get to Birmingham they will (for a small fee of course!) do your desk research for you.

A similar service is available from the British Library Business Information Service in London. Again, see the Appendix.

Local Authorities

Most local authorities produce, annually, some form of 'economic assessment' for their area. It will help you to find out local trends with housing, employment and much more. This should be available in the local library, but if not check with the economic development section within your local authority. While you are at it, ask them for any other information that they may have to help you with your research. For example, they usually hold a vacant commercial property database, which could help you in your search for premises.

Newspapers
Keep an eye out in both national and local press for snippets of useful information. Often papers will reproduce a survey from large market research firms, and this could put you in the right direction for answers to your questions.

Internet
There is a vast amount of information available on the internet – the problem is sifting through the dross. (See the Appendix.)

Business Link
Check out the Growth and Improvement Service pages of the Business Link website for useful information (see the Appendix).

Enterprise Agencies
They often have good business start-up advisers who will give you free advice. Their localized knowledge will be invaluable and a session with them will get your research moving rapidly. Again, see the Appendix for their website address.

The Competition
Every business has competition. So check on yours, become a 'bogus' customer and ask them for a quotation, check their prices and resources. What are they good and bad at and do their weak areas present you with an opportunity? You may, of course, be working for your future competition and planning to set up yourself!

Existing Customers
If you are an established business, never stop asking your existing customers questions about your product or service. What do they expect from you and can you provide it? Look after this lot, as it is far easier to sell to existing customers – use them as your sales force and value the input and

contribution they can make to your on-going research. Listen to them and learn; be serious about customer care. You will spend time and good money on winning their custom in the first place, so put just as much effort into keeping them. But we digress, back to market research!

Surveys
This isn't easy for some people. But you will need to get answers straight from your potential customers.

If you are employed in the sector you plan to launch your own venture in, then you will have been in contact (discreetly of course!) with your potential customers, and your surveying is fairly straightforward. Mind you, it is often surprising just how many budding entrepreneurs fail to understand how much research they already have in front of them!

If not, gird your loins, and get asking those questions. Often start-ups fear this aspect of research because they are concerned that they may be letting their proposed venture out of the bag and alerting their competition to a threat in their backyard. But, the world has to know about you at some stage, so get asking. Who and where are your potential customers? Well, your desk research should have answered that one, and if you want to remain anonymous then get someone else to do the asking – more on this on page 73.

Observation
If your competition can be seen and watched, then do it. See what they stock, ask assistants questions and they will inadvertently offer up valuable information the owner or manager would be more reluctant to volunteer. As previously mentioned, get the competition to give you a quotation (for fictitious work, of course) and, if you are not sure who or where the competition is, why not place an advertisement asking for what you are planning to offer? That way you may get responses from competitors that you didn't know existed. (For example, if you are thinking of offering a book-keeping service, then place a classified advert in the local paper asking for a book-keeper, and so on.) I'm sure you have got the gist.

Experiment

Get samples out and ask for feedback. Yes, try friends and family but be cautious of their responses as they may find it difficult in telling you that the 'greatest thing since sliced bread' is rubbish. Try to get to potential customers for more realistic feedback.

Example of Market Research

Well, I hear you saying, this is all very well but how does this theory apply to the real world? Fair question, so here is an example of it in action. This is from a recent start-up that eventually entered the landscaping sector.

They are a partnership, one partner was working part-time in landscaping and the other was unemployed. Both were keen and determined to get started, yet practical enough to understand the importance of research.

Their first port of call was their local library to check out:

Competition

They looked through landscaping trade directories, Yellow Pages and local press, which of course confirmed what one partner already knew from working part-time in the industry.

Local Authority

To see their available research and get an indication on housing types from checking the council tax bands in the area. This helped to find out the number of properties over a certain size and possibly with large gardens.

Local Authority Economic Assessment

This indicated the local plans about new housing and business support in the area.

Having armed themselves with this desk research they then obtained the relevant Business Opportunities Profiles and Fact Sheets from the local banks, while checking on the banks' latest deals for new business accounts!

Competition
An obliging friend with a neglected garden asked their potential competitors for quotations. Typically, of course, some even failed to turn up to give a quote: suggesting they were either too busy – so there was plenty of work about – or more likely they couldn't care less and the words 'customer care' weren't part of their vocabulary!

Garden Centres
They visited local garden centres to check out if a referral service was an option. While this produced mixed results it did lead to a couple of promising contacts for potential suppliers.

Leaflets/Questionnaires
These were dropped by the two partners through the doors of 1,000 potential customers. This yielded 40 positive responses and encouraged the budding entrepreneurs – no horticultural pun intended. Yes, they were exhausted after this exercise but they fully appreciated that their livelihood depended on finding customers. Incidentally, the questionnaire asked what clients wanted and were prepared to pay in addition to questions about their competition. Who designed the questionnaire? All will be revealed at the end of this chapter!

Pubs
Not a bad idea to have another stiff drink at this stage, is it? But our two fearless entrepreneurs had an idea that local publicans might need a good, reliable landscaping service. They came up with the idea of adding a design and build service, to incorporate features like barbecues that landlords could use in the summer months. This part of their field research was enjoyable but only yielded a mixed response.

Armed with their information they then calculated how much 'potential' work there was, their hourly rate, how many hours they could realistically work in a typical month, checked their survival income, and what they needed to borrow to get started. They placed it all into a coherent business plan, highlighting their market research and set about visiting the main funding source for start-ups – the high street banks. The first one turned them down because of a poor credit rating for the unemployed partner. But these guys were determined and asked another bank, which agreed to fund their venture.

How are they doing? At the time of writing they started six years ago. They now employ three full-timers, are making a reasonable profit and have not looked back. It has been hard work but their determination has seen them through. By the way, the idea for the pubs turned out to be a non-starter. The domestic market has kept them busy enough. To get them going they linked up with a housing developer. Plus they ride on the back of those numerous gardening makeover programmes on television. Oh and yes, they did landscape their friend's neglected garden – as a thank you!

How did they crack it?

These gardeners didn't just link up with the property developer but became an integral part of its service to its buyers. How? They became the garden problem solvers for the developer's clients.

Within the developer's housing there were properties ranging from starter homes to large detached houses. The purchasers had different needs when it came to the garden.

Our intrepid start-ups realised this and offered different packages to each type of home buyer. For starter home buyers, where cash was tight, they offered a DIY package, consisting of plants and a plan the customer could implement himself.

In contrast, the detached-home buyers were offered a full supply, plant and maintenance service.

Is there a way you could offer a choice of packages to your range of clients?

Hopefully, this example illustrates how straightforward and essential market research can be. It is easy to get bogged down and make it complicated, particularly at the desk research stage. While this example may not relate to your business and appear too localised, just scale the process up or down according to your requirements.

Throughout this chapter there have been references to a source of help with your market research, so, here it is: contact the nearest university or college. They will have students, on marketing courses, desperate to carry out real research as evidence for their qualifications. Offer a prize or some other incentive and they will roar away at the research for you. The questionnaire the potential landscapers distributed was drawn up by marketing students for them. They didn't have a clue how to phrase the questions and worked closely with a group of students to produce the questionnaire, and then distributed it themselves.

Market research isn't and needn't be difficult, but it is essential – so do it!

Then have a stiff drink and . . . go for it!

5

THE MARKETING AND SELLING OF YOU

Well done, you made it through the research and money bits now you deserve some fun.

How about the selling stuff? Well, believe it or not some of you may fear this even more than the money stuff! Or, heaven forbid, have the attitude that selling is going to be easy because everybody wants your product or service. Ouch! There -- did you feel that smack from the book to bring you back to your senses?

All too often the self-employed, and particularly those new to self-employment, fail to grasp just how important marketing and selling is to the success or failure of their venture.

Marketing is something the 'big boys' do. And as for selling, well the attitude is either it is 'easy to sell', because 'everybody wants what I am offering', or 'I will be cheaper than the big boys, so I am bound to get plenty of orders.'

Wakey wakey!

The first principle to grasp is:

WHAT ARE THE SELF-EMPLOYED ACTUALLY MARKETING AND SELLING?

In the words of an infamous TV show you are allowed to ask a friend, ask the audience, or take a fifty-fifty on this one! Whatever you decide, the answer had better be 'THEMSELVES'.

Yes, you will have a product or service you are offering the world, but unless **YOU** get out there and market and sell YOU, failure waits around the corner.

Right from the start promote YOU and your image: work on it, refine it, and develop it because in the first year of trading this is going to be your most effective marketing tool – YOU!

Your background might include working for a large organisation, and your role in that organisation may well have been in the marketing or sales sections, so you may be well versed in the principles and theories of marketing. But as soon as you go self-employed the marketing support machine is no longer available to you. Brochures, telephone support, mail-shots, quotes and all the rest of the paraphernalia that such a machine can use promoting and selling its 'empire' will be down to little old you. Yes, self-employment puts the emphasis on the 'self'!

It isn't rocket science

A couple of years ago our washing machine decided to break down.

I called a repair business and they said they would come around 2 pm to have a look at it.

First winning action – he turned up on time, neat and polite.

He diagnosed the problem and said he would have to go for a part but be back in half an hour.

Second winning action – he was.

The part was fitted, he checked everything worked. He then pulled a sticker from his pocket and placed it on the washing machine. 'If it ever goes wrong again, there is my phone number on the sticker.'

Easy, isn't it? He made it easy for me should it break down again.

Guess what? This guy was self-employed and had realised customer loyalty and referals were vital to his business.

What is Marketing?

I ask this on all start-up courses and wait with bated breath for the answer. Why? Well, on one course a voice shouted out 'lying' and I even started to write it up on the whiteboard. Worse still, he wasn't joking. Needless to say that turned out to be an interesting session! No, the response I often get is 'selling' for which I thank the Lord for delivering them into my hands.

Marketing
Sales with a college education.
John Freund

There is a difference between marketing and selling and this is why some businesses get into problems with both. They confuse themselves, but worst still they confuse their customers by giving out mixed messages. The trouble is, some of the big boys get the two mixed up. They will employ a 'sales and marketing' manager. Heck I have worked with plenty of people who were good at one but lousy at the other – it was usually selling they were worse at, by the way.

One definition for marketing is giving customers what they want, when they want, and at a price that makes you both happy. A shorter one is the application of common sense. Good old common sense, something we all claim to have loads of – really? It is a constant source of amazement just how hard some businesses make it for potential customers to be able to deal with them. How about this as an example of a common sense approach to marketing by a self-employed start-up:

An ex-directory phone number for the business.

And they couldn't understand why clients found it hard to reach them!

No doubt your marketing budget will be tight (please don't say it is non-existent), so you need to be innovative and cost-effective in your approach to marketing yourself. One of the first things to grasp is that you should never miss an opportunity to market or sell 'you'.

Communication is going to be your biggest marketing tool, so use it right from the start of your venture. Come up with an unusual angle or story on your start-up and get that information out to all the relevant media to promote your launch. A quick tip: sometimes it is wise not to put the words 'new business' in your details, but use something like 'After two years in development this product/service is now available.' This avoids the natural suspicion we humans have of something new.

Marketing
The stuff I do that makes my phone ring.
Anon

On the other hand, if your product or service is aimed at the buyers that like to be in first and get their hands-on the latest gizmos, 'new' will of course be a trigger word. But what is 'new' about another painter and decorator? In that case you need to get your potential clients believing in your experience. See the next chapter on promotion for more on this topic.

Send out letters to potential customers and stop putting on the typical large organisation comment: 'Don't hesitate to contact us if you need more information.' What a great way to kill a sale! Tell them you will ring them in seven days to discuss the contents in more detail. If you are going to be sending out hundreds of letters to potential clients, then identify those that are the main targets and tell them you will be ringing, or send them out in batches. And, make sure you do ring otherwise a reputation for being unreliable will start sticking to your name.

Every correspondence you send out will convey an image to the recipients; make sure the image they build up of you encourages rather than discourages them from using you.

Oh, yes, and try to avoid overuse of Microsoft's idea of

'business' clip art! Be clear and precise with all your communication – even with your payment terms!

One bright start-up places a simple flyer in every item of
correspondence sent – even invoices. As he pointed out 'You
never know who might read it – especially in a large organisation.'

This leads us on to an area the self-employed can score over
the 'big boys':

Customer Care

Change those two words to 'Good Service' and apply them
zealously to all of your dealings with potential and existing
clients. Don't be like the crowd of businesses that make a
token effort towards customer care – make sure you mean it.
You will have gone to great lengths to find and get customers,
so devote just as much effort, if not more, to keeping them.
Stand by your word, become reliable and an essential part of
your customers' lives and they will turn into your sales force
by promoting and selling to others for you. There you go –
how to set up a sales team for nothing!

Have you ever gone into a shop and suddenly realised that
you have switched into invisible mode again? Now I know we
don't want sales staff all over us – well, not until we are ready to
do the deal, anyway. But a simple acknowledgment of our existence might be appreciated. I recently went into a card shop to
get a Good Luck card for one of my clients (because I know how
to look after them!). I chose the card I wanted but couldn't find
the correct envelope for it. At the till the two sales assistants
were deep into some gossip and I was a potential threat to their
flow of drivel. So, they thought, best ignore him and then he
might go away. But I am made of tougher stuff and held my
ground. Grudgingly they both stopped and looked at me. I asked
for an envelope and the look they gave each other spoke
volumes. 'Bloody customers' oozed from their body language.
But I was still determined to see it through. They found an
envelope and rang the item into the till. I asked for some stamps.
'We don't sell them,' with a look of disgust from the assistant. I
shook my head, left the card and went to another card shop.

They never cried out for me to return and probably looked at each other and said 'bloody customers'. Guess what I will be saying locally about that card shop? Be positive in any selling situation. More on this in a moment.

A Word of Warning about Marketing

Marketing can become a way to stroke your own vanity or ego. Flash cards and leaflets, a fancy website or whatever can take over. Just keep asking yourself: will this activity lead to sales? Don't get me wrong, I want you to present a good image – but think your marketing plans through.

Back when I was in the wholesale horticultural world I recall asking the sales manager of a competitor why they were at an exhibition. He replied, 'Well we have got to wave the flag, haven't we?'

No, I think not. He was there to generate leads and get business. That way your firm can keep providing you with that fancy company car you bore us all about.

See what I mean about the different mindset of the employed?

Selling

Selling can, for some of those new to self-employment, be surrounded with mystery and trepidation. Well, it shouldn't, because you have been doing it for years without realising it! Try using the word 'negotiating' instead of 'selling'. When you asked for an increase in pocket money, or salary, you were selling yourself. Watch children asking their parents for a new toy – talk about high-powered selling skills!

Refine those skills, learn to accept that word 'no' as just two little old letters and in the words of the song, 'Dust yourself off and start all over again'. Resilience will be a great selling tool so learn to use it right from the start.

Selling
A man without a smiling face should not open shop.
Chinese Proverb

What other selling 'tools' can you use? Well, enthusiasm is one of the greatest selling tools around – though it appears a rare commodity in some shop salespeople! Though most of them are not selling, just taking orders and there is a big difference. The self-employed will often be drawn to a business idea from something they are interested in, consequently they will possess an in-built enthusiasm about the product or service. You've got it so you should use it, and it is a great selling tool.

The Determination Tale

I was working with two landscape gardening start-up businesses – and the contrast between the two couldn't have been greater.

Both of them were well trained, knew their plants, having worked in the trade for several years. But that is where the similarity ended.

Maria was determined to make her venture work. Whereas Alan thought it would be a doddle – 'plenty of work for landscapers' he kept saying to me.

They were both giving out quotes to potential clients. And they were both losing and not picking up the work.

Alan just shrugged his shoulders and implied it was the stupid clients' fault that he wasn't getting the work.

Not Maria. She realised that you need to be more proactive. She picked up the phone and asked, in a polite way, what was wrong with her quote.

And sure enough she discovered that clients don't compare like with like when looking at a quote, but just look at the prices quoted.

Maria changed her approach and wouldn't just pop a quote in the post and hope for the best. Not Maria; she would take the quote to potential clients and talk them through her pricing. She emphasised the quality of materials, etc.

The work started to come in. Alan? He gave up and went back to the world of the employed.

Selling Needs Belief in Yourself
Do you know who this was?

Ran for the legislature and lost in 1832.
Had nervous breakdown in 1836.
Defeated for Congress in 1843.
Defeated for Congress in 1846.
Defeated for Congress in 1848.
Defeated for the Senate in 1855.
Defeated for Vice-President in 1856.
Elected President of the United States in 1860.

The man was Abraham Lincoln.

Here is a collection of random tips from other business start-ups that may just help you to stand out from the crowd and win more business.

Be Positive
It sounds ever so corny but a negative approach breeds negativity! If you are providing your customers with a solution, then don't sound like you are creating more problems for them. For example, when you say, 'We've sold out', be careful – you are in negative mode. Add 'We are expecting more on Friday, would you like me to save you one?' That's much more positive and it gives the customer a possible solution. Or you may suggest an 'alternative' product as a solution. In short, don't cause customers' problems! I remember watching aghast as one shopkeeper proudly said that he didn't take credit cards without offering the customer an alternative method of payment. And then moaned when she walked out of the shop leaving the goods on the counter.

Become The Problem Solver
What business problem does your client need solving?

High Overheads
Staffing
Equipment
Competition
Budgeting
Targets

Offer to solve their problems.
   See the panel on page 72 for how a gardening business came up with solutions for their clients.

Keep Customers on Your Side
How many times do you go into a shop and feel you have suddenly become invisible? Well, we self-employed retailers would never treat a customer like that, would we? Of course not. If you are busy, at least acknowledge the customer's existence and say you will be with him or her as soon as you can.

Procrastination
Tomorrow is the day on which lazy people have the most to do.
Norwegian Proverb

Use the Telephone as a Friend
When the phone rings, do you think of it as an interruption or another opportunity to sell? Well, it will depend on your type of business I suppose, but generally it should be an opportunity to do some selling. (Though unless you are good at it selling on the phone is hard. Look on it as an opportunity to get an appointment.)

It never ceases to amaze me the number of self-employed who don't have an answerphone or a mobile. And when they do, they still make it difficult for their customers. This is one of my hobby horses – the telephone. Or more precisely the way too many of the self-employed fail to grasp how important the phone is to their business. And, if you work from home and use the same line for business and domestic purposes, make sure the other members of your family answer professionally. I rang one start-up to get a quote to be told by a child that 'He is on the toilet.' One of the weirdest examples I have of this is the start-up who had this message on his mobile: 'Sorry my message service isn't working so please send me a text.' Oh where, oh where, do I begin with this one? Let's jump the reality chasm – suffice it to say that 'end' is a better word than 'begin'.

The Phone
If you are nervous about a particular phone call you have to make, then **stand up** when on the phone. You will sound much more positive and, if you pace about as well, the brain will click more readily into gear!

Make the Sale Bigger
Simple this – if you sell shoes think of all the extras you could sell: polish, laces. It will look like you care and you will increase the value of the sale to you. And on that point, why don't bookshops sell reading glasses?

Don't be a Delivery Optimist
When promising to deliver, either make sure you can keep to the deadline or, even better still, ring up early and say that the order is ready now. There was a very successful engineering business that stated on all order confirmations that, if they were an hour late in delivering, the customer got the goods for free! Did it ever happen? Yes, apparently, once and they had

to honour this pledge. Remember: you may not be able to compete on price but you can beat the big boys on service!

Get Referrals
Use your existing customers as your sales team. Ask them for referrals. Perhaps give them an incentive to recommend you. Network with a business that deals with similar customers to the ones you seek and share out business cards. Though be careful not to 'dilute' your message and be sure you can trust the other business to give your customers as good a service as you do!

Get Paid
A sale is not a sale until it's ordered, delivered and paid for – and the cheque has cleared or the cash is in your hand. Always remember that your business is not money-lending and if customers are bad payers – tell them!

Listen
Listen to what your customers, both potential and existing, say to you, and respond accordingly. Use your contacts and get information from them about potential sales leads. Be honest, don't promise what you can't deliver – remember that 'image' that you have spent ages in cultivating and promoting in your marketing? Well, it has just been shot down in flames by letting that customer down, and they will have great pleasure in telling people how bad you are.

Plan the selling 'campaign' – don't waste your valuable time. Rehearse your 'pitch', get out there and use it. Alter it, amend and be adaptable. Believe in yourself and your product or service. All of this may sound very stirring, but you must get motivated – if you can't, self-employment is not going to work for you. Do you still need motivation to sell? Check your survival income and that will focus you!

But the biggest selling tool? Well, there are two really. First: satisfied customers; in other words, word of mouth. But don't let word of mouth become an excuse for not doing any promotion. Remember that when you start in business you are the mouth that needs to spread the word. Satisfied customers don't talk as much as dissatisfied ones (there is a rule in there somewhere, and I reckon it is simply as a nation we like to 'have a good moan'), so make sure your customers are happy! Common sense, really!

And secondly . . .

Ask for the Business
Don't be afraid to ask for the business. Don't be afraid to ask for the business. Don't be afraid to ask for the business. Don't be afraid to ask for the business. Don't be afraid to ask for the business. *Get the message?*

It is amazing how much effort will go into all the preceding bits. Your marketing will be superb, second to none; your image will be a shining example to PR consultants. You will negotiate your way into the customers' premises, listen to them, and ask the right questions – except that last and most important one, 'Are you going to give me the darned order?' All that hard work flies straight out of the window. You fear that word 'no'. Well don't. Get used to it, but don't give up.

Sell the Benefits
People buy what something will do for them – sorry to state the obvious! Some start-ups though get so bogged down with the features that they lose business.

When you buy a new television, you don't ask about the stuff inside the box. You want to know how it can improve your entertainment experience.

You buy fuel for your car – not for the experience of putting it in your car, but to get where you want to be!

The grass box on my mower is a feature but the benefit is a tidier lawn.

Fiat Cars used to run two versions of the same TV advertisement. One aimed at the male market and the other at the female market.

The female version featured a man in the driving seat. He explained to the camera that the car comes with power steering. 'Which means it is easy for you girls to park.'

The male version had a pretty girl in the driving seat. She looked at the camera and pouted about it having such and such gizmo under the bonnet. 'Which means that you can impress your mates.'

OK, not very subtle but at least they had identified the benefits to the different sectors.

Business Names

Business names are another good marketing/selling tool. One of my hobbies is collecting unusual business names (well, we all have to have a hobby!), and opposite is a sample. To check out the legal side about choosing a business name refer to Chapter 8.

Tag Lines

Tag lines on your promotional material can be a good sales tool. How about adding some humour, like these examples?

Outside a bric a brac shop:
We buy junk and sell antiques
Outside an exhaust dealer:
No appointment necessary. We'll hear you coming . . .
In a vet's waiting room:
Be back in 5 minutes. Sit! Stay!
Plumber:
We repair what your husband fixed.
That last one could be used by most tradesmen!

Balti Towers	Indian restaurant, Dudley, West Midlands.
Farm Assist	Farm chemical supplies, Herefordshire.
Tanz-n-ere	Tanning shop, Broxbourne, Hertfordshire.
Knobs & Knockers	Door shop, Chelsea, London.
Suite FA	Sofa shop, Finchley, London.
Iron Maidens	Ironing service, Ross on Wye.
The Codfather	Fish and chip shop, Brighton.
Sam Widges	Sandwich shop, Holborn, London.
British Gnome Stores	Gnome shop, Devon.
Pizza the Action	Pizza restaurant, Fulham, London.
Spread 'Em	Sandwich shop, Bristol
Athlete's Foot	Sports shop, Limassol, Cyprus.
Sure Lock Homes	Locksmiths, Torbay, Devon.

A Wee Bit of Psychology

To understand how you sell, you need to understand why your customers buy from you – and to grasp this you need to start with what type of business you are in.

Generally, there are three types of business: Service-, Product- or a Price-led business.

Service-led

Virgin and the supermarket Waitrose are two examples of service-led businesses. They do not chase the lowest price but offer exceptional service and quality. They can't offer both because their service level would be reduced. Next time you fly out of Heathrow see how the red-coated Virgin staff care for their customers.

Product-led

Apple and Nokia are two examples of product-led companies. They strive to produce the best products in their field. They know that their customers want the latest (and probably most fashionable) product. Their customers will pay a premium for their products – but they expect the best.

Price-led

EasyJet, Ryan Air and Lidl are examples of price-led companies. They aim to offer the lowest possible price to their customer. Their clients will forgo extras and consequently the budget airline passenger doesn't expect free refreshments onboard.

So which are you? Do you understand what you are offering your clients? What's in it for them? What do they expect from you? People buy the *benefit* of your business to them, not the *features* of your business. You'll come up with loads of features about your business. Look at each one and ask yourself what it means to customers.

As a crude example, a lawn mower (there we go, getting all horticultural again) with a grass box (feature) provides the buyer with a tidier lawn – the benefit!

Amazon clearly knows what its business is about. Amazon staff have little or no face-to-face contact with their customer. The feature of their business is the backroom software and service – the benefit to you is that they put you in complete control of the buying process.

Features and Benefits

For some people, selling can be one of the hardest parts in establishing and running their new business. A clear understanding of just what it is you are selling, and what your customers expect when they buy from you, will help overcome this problem. The features and benefits principle is as old as the hills. But hey don't knock it – it works!

List the features of your product or service and then place a benefit to your customers alongside it, in the benefits column.

When you have a feature ask, SO WHAT? or WHICH MEANS THAT? and WHAT IS IN IT FOR MY CUSTOMERS?

Don't just keep putting 'saves money' as a benefit! Now you have the benefits and understand your customers' needs better, you can start to produce your sales literature, advertisements and so on. Concentrate on these benefits and SELL them to your customers.

UNDERSTAND CLEARLY WHAT YOUR CUSTOMERS WANT FROM YOU.

Having cracked the features and benefits bit, then try to answer other questions your customers might have:

WHY YOU? WHAT IS SPECIAL ABOUT YOU? WHY SHOULD I COME TO YOU?

Look at those benefits and understand why customers will buy from you.

Use this table to compile your own features and benefits list.

Feature	Benefit	Which means for the customer?

That Word 'No!'

It has already been said that you are going to get 'no's' when selling – so get used to them and learn from them.

When prospective clients say 'no', ask for further information. They may say, 'You are too expensive.' Well, seek enlightenment!

Are they really comparing like with like? Stress the benefits to them.

They may be happy with their current supplier, in which case don't knock your competition, it just isn't professional. Concentrate on how you are different, and ask them, maybe, if they would consider a trial order.

If they won't give you the order, back off and suggest you contact them again in a number of weeks – put it in your diary and do it!

Just Interested

In my early days in sales I had a Sales Manager who would constantly say to me, 'Never bring me just interested.' In other words, that is 'work in progress' which he knew we had in hand. He wanted firm orders. Mind you the Finance Manager would always add 'even that doesn't matter until the bill is paid and money is in the bank'.

They were right – don't get carried away with 'just interested'. Some potential clients will say that to get rid of you and backtrack at a later date. Like 'no' get used to this – it's business!

Networking

And finally, make business contacts – networking in modern terminology. Get yourself to breakfast networking clubs (though they do start inordinately early in the day!), or trade seminars. Mix, mingle and keep your ears and eyes open.

6

YOUR PROMOTIONAL CHOICES

Advertising

It never ceases to amaze me how people without any previous marketing skills believe they know how to produce good promotional material.

Suddenly, because they have become self-employed, overnight they can master talents that they have never needed in their life.

You wouldn't dream of starting your businesses without getting some financial advice, would you? (If you would, then close this book now and hit yourself on the head, very hard, with it.)

Suddenly we are highly talented advertising gurus; second to none, in fact, at producing powerful copy and advertisements.

Think again. All too often the result is a hotchpotch produced on a home PC, dripping with clip art and destined straight for the recipient's dustbin.

Harsh words?

Well, perhaps the following examples will prove my point. To protect the guilty their details have been blacked out – though they don't really deserve to be anonymous.

Overleaf is a real example presented to me by a potential start-up. It is reproduced accurately, including the spelling mistake. And please, what does 'no job too small' mean? Can someone explain what they think they are conveying with that expression? Desperation is what I see – certainly not professionalism.

> **All Gardening work done.**
> Turf
> Pruning
> Ponds
> Tree Work
>
> No job to small
>
> Call
> 07777 777777

When I started to talk to this potential horticultural wizard it was clear he knew his trade. He was qualified and experienced. So tell the prospective clients that! How about this for an alternative approach?

> ## Trees, Shrubs, Weeds and Tubs.
>
> Name your gardening problem – there is a solution.
>
> From design to maintenance – with years of experience.
>
> And satisfied clients to prove it.
>
> To arrange a **FREE** no obligation meeting simply ring
> (Business Name Here)
>
> ### 01999 123456

Now, OK, it won't win a Design Council award. A graphic designer could come up with something snazzier with all the right typefaces and graphics. Instead of a black background top and bottom, green would probably be a better gardening business colour. But it is better, isn't it?

The attention grabber is at the top with a clear call to action, and the phone number is also highlighted. Experience is now mentioned, plus satisfied customers to back up your claims. 'But I haven't got any customers, let alone satisfied ones.' Are you telling me you are starting this business venture without having 'tested' your idea and skills on somebody? Not even a family member or friend? Well, if you haven't yet, then make me this promise: you will test your skills out on someone. Then ask for feedback. Listen and act on their view of you and your work. If they like you – voilà, you have the first 'satisfied client' to act as your sales force. But graphic designers are expensive, so if your start-up funds are low then you could try the following.

Is there a local art college you could approach to get a design for business cards, etc.? Offer a prize for the winning design. Then take your design to a local printer to run up. Check your competition. Is there something you can 'borrow' from their promotional material? Local papers will often help with your advertisement wording and layout. Though beware, they will tell you 'size matters' and try to run up your modest budget.

How about this example from the classified section of a local paper?

CHEAP
REPAIRS

WASHING MACHINES

COOKERS

FRIDGES

(01999) 123456

Short and to the point. But further down the page was a direct competitor.

REPAIRS TO
WASHING MACHINES
TUMBLE DRYERS
COOKERS etc.

No call out charge
Same day service
wherever possible.
Tel:
SOMETOWN
DOMESTICS
on (01999) 543210
or 07777 123456

On start-up courses I will often hand out the page from the paper and ask which one clients prefer. Now I don't think I have to intimidate them too much into choosing the second one!

It is better simply because it addresses customer concerns. 'No call out charge' and I will get to you the same day if I can. Also a couple of phone numbers to reach me on – making it easier for you to contact me. The daft thing is that both classifieds are the same size, so they will cost the same to insert. But who do you reckon gets the better return on their promotional budget? I watched this section of the paper for a few months. And guess what? The 'Cheap Repairs' character disappeared while the other is still there.

Moral of this tale? Get your promotion right, repeat it, test it – but most of all keep doing it.

Clever Clogs?
Catch All
Some clever clogs actually place two adverts with a different contact number on each to try to catch both ends of the potential market!

Yellow Pages
One start-up small builder told me proudly how he had allocated his annual advertising budget in one easy stroke: 'Put it all into Yellow Pages.' Just one drawback, he was talking to me in April and Yellow Pages update and come out in September. He had six months of no exposure! Watch those Yellow Pages salespeople. They are very good at their selling job.

Yellow Pages or Thomson?
Thomson is more local – it concentrates on dialing codes. Whereas Yellow Pages is more widespread. So be sure you are in the right one. If your target area is 20 miles or so, maybe Thomson will be more effective for you.

Emphasise Local

If there is room in your advert it is a good idea to include your address or location. Nowadays when local papers cover such wide areas, the customer often wants to know exactly where a tradesman is based.

Spend Wisely

Ask any publication you are considering advertising in for their 'media pack'. It will show readership numbers and profiles of the readers.

Negotiate Rates

Never accept the rate to advertise that is first offered to you. Haggle to get it down. I have seen reductions of up to 50 per cent.

Position

Top right-hand corner is the best place to position your press adverts. Even better, try to get on the TV listings page.

Repeat, Repeat . . .

You need to keep repeating your adverts. Potential clients need to see you again and again for reassurance!

Size

Size may not matter and, if your budget is tight, many small repeat adverts may work better for you.

Magic Words

The following words are the ones you need to get in the headlines of your promotional material:

Free
You
Your
Discover
New
How
How to
Easy
Why
Wanted
Save
Secret
Offer
Bargain

Try different ones and see which one strikes the best chord with clients.

Never Use 'We'

Apparently it isn't a good idea to put all your headlines in CAPITALS. Try to vary them with Title Case – Which Is Like This. Also use a serif font; they have twiddly bits on the letters and are easier to read.

Put your main benefit first and avoid emblazing it with your business name; unless it says what you do for your customer, such as . . .

Speedy Computer Repairs
which is much better than D B Services. That means nothing to anybody.

South West Technology
is too vague. What on earth do they do?

A Word About 'Word of Mouth'

'Word of mouth will get me plenty of business.' Those words always make me shudder when I hear them from potential business start-ups. When you start out YOU are the mouth that has to create the word. Agreed, it is one of the best forms of business promotion but don't fall into the trap of making it an excuse for not doing any promotion.

In the world of advertising the following saying is attributed to Lord Lever (he of the washing-up liquid). 'Half of my advertising is a waste of money – the trouble is I don't know which half.' This is then blown up by some start-ups into believing that all promotion is going to be a waste of money. And becomes, 'I'll just get some cheap business cards and flyers and that'll do.' In our self-employed world we should know what has been an effective promotional method or not. Here's a simple solution: ask new or potential customers the following. 'How did you get to hear about us?' Start noting this whenever you ring an existing business and see if they ask you this question. I would bet that you will hardly ever hear it. Why? They have become complacent and probably don't care about you and your potential business. More about looking after your customers later.

AIDA

In the world of advertising, this is as old as the hills. But, hey, don't knock it – it works. Whenever you produce some promotional material, give it the AIDA test. It goes like this . . .

Attention

It should grab the reader's attention. Use a picture or those magic words opposite. You have nano seconds to make an impression.

Interest

Make sure you answer the 'What's in it for me?' question from the reader. Use facts or quotes to back up what you are saying.

Desire
Bit of a naff word, but what you want to get the reader saying is 'without this product or service, my life is but nought'. Use everyday but inspiring language.

Action
Get all the above right but you can still fail at this last hurdle. Make it easy for them to contact you. It never ceases to amaze me how often phone numbers are missing from promotional literature. If you make it hard for them, potential clients will go elsewhere. They always have another choice!

Please **proof read** any material you produce or have produced. One client had 5,000 leaflets printed and didn't spot that the word 'chair' appeared as 'choir'. Whoops!

So, there you sit wondering what choices you may have when it comes to promotion.

You may have jotted down some of the following: flyers, posters, business cards, shop windows, classifieds, advert in the press (pause for breath), T-shirts, baseball caps, balloons, beer mats, local radio, local TV, editorials, buses (another pause for breath), Yellow Pages, Thomson, trade directories, trade magazines, internet, exhibitions, sponsorship, carrier bags, mailshots . . .

But Where Do You Begin?
Start by looking at where your competitors do their promotion. Time has hopefully told them which options work and which don't. Now I know they could fall into that complacent mob that I had a go at before, but they won't all be like that. So, ring them up pretending to be interested in doing business with them. String them along. Then gently go in for the killer question. 'Oh, by the way I saw your advert/flyer/business card in xxxxx, I bet you get loads of calls from that?' And if

Signs

Shop and vehicle signs can, of course, be a great promotional tool – but not in these two cases. These are real examples!

Dry Cleaning Shop
Same Day Cleaning
All
Garments
Ready in
48 Hours

Builders
Our Motto:
We Promise
You The
Lowest
Prices
and Workmanship

Clothing

This can help promote your business. I will never forget the time I travelled by train to Plymouth. This bloke kept walking up and down the train with 'Devonsailing.com' emblazoned on his sweatshirt. All those passengers heading to the West Country on holiday certainly got the message.

A singer I worked with produced beer mats displaying her name and contact details. The first thing she did when arriving at a gig was to remove all the existing beer mats on the tables and replace them with hers.

Also, why don't all tradespeople have signs to place outside a property where they are doing work? For example, a landscape gardener should have a sign saying 'Garden currently being transformed by XXXXX Landscapes'.

stuck for inspiration adapt (I didn't say copy) their material. Tweak it and make it yours and get it out. Test it. Did it work? No, then change it and try again. You know what Shakespeare said about once more into the breach!

Never forget that people don't buy a paper to read the adverts. They want news, and information. They want to know what's on the box and the football results. Your wonderful ego-boosting advert is noticed purely by chance!

Free Newspapers
Weigh up if you want to be in those free publications that come through your letterbox. How often do *you* read them? It is probably better to be in a paid-for paper that people will actually read rather than wind up in the bin.

Using the press
I recall that one start-up setting up as a pawnbroker found that local bylaws prevented him from setting up in certain parts of his town. He expanded it into 'The Council won't let me start my pawnbroker business' article.

For four weeks running he was on the front page of the local paper and when he finally opened he was on the front again.

A non-story but it worked.

Incidentally, try doing a cash flow for that type of business. You have stock but you don't have stock!

Be Different
One small independent garden centre used to run a series of adverts with this heading:
   Can You Spot Four Things Wrong With This Picture?
   The picture would be changed monthly and feature some product used incorrectly or a pest munching at a plant. To get the answer you had to call into the garden centre.

Business Cards

If you move in a sector that expects business cards to be handed out as the norm, then always give someone two cards. Say one is for the recipient and the other is to pass on in case he or she meets someone else who needs your product or service.

See the Appendix for details of a website producing competitively priced business cards and leaflets.

Letters

Will you be sending letters out to drum up trade? Well, as is typical of this book here is an example of how not to do it. This letter came to our office and was trying to sell us a service to offer our clients. It read:

Dear Sirs,

I know how annoying junk mail can be and I apologise for what you might regard as a bit more, but I hope that what I can offer you is something worthwhile. If not then throw this away and I wont bother you again.

As you can see from the enclosed leaflet, my services are aimed at small to medium sizes businesses which do not want to finance an employee for doing all the tiresome book-keeping and wages, so what generally happens is the owner does it themselves then passes it all over to an accountant at the end of each year. The accountant will look over it and inform you of any taxes which need paying. This does not keep you informed on a month to month basis.

I will do much more than that. I will take all your book-keeping and or wages every month and present you with a full statement of facts which we can go over together and look for any problems so we can catch them early.

My costs are lower than you might think, all pricing is based on the amount of time the job takes, if you have a lot of paperwork then it takes longer than a business which has a little. I will agree a price with you before we start and I will hold this firm for 12 months and probably not increase it after that, its important to me to keep you happy and successful.

I currently have businesses which turn over £60,000 and some which turnover a million, I treat them all the same, they are all important.

I want you to be successful, I will advise and help in whatever way I can, but my intention is to not interfere with the way you run your business.

Yours sincerely

Principle

This terrible letter!
Oh where to begin . . .

Dear Sirs
Well, they can't even be bothered to find out to whom to address the letter.

I know how annoying junk mail can be
Yup, I agree; this is annoying junk mail so I will bin it. Don't start on a negative.

As you can see from the enclosed leaflet
No leaflet was enclosed. And how about a pause for breath? Look at the size of this paragraph.
Bad move: don't criticise the opposition.

I will do much more than that
I, I, I. This letter is all about him! There are over 18 references to 'I', 'me' and 'my'. Only eight about 'you'.

Probably not increase
Gee, thanks.

I currently have
Me, me, me again!

I want you to be successful
Thanks. Don't worry pal – you are coming nowhere near my business.

And to end: a stupid spelling mistake

And finally. Try to avoid ending an introductory letter with 'Please don't hesitate to contact us.' If you are sending out small quantities of targeted mail then tell them you will ring them 'in five days to see how we can work together to help your business grow'.

Quotations

Why do people make quotations look and sound so dreary? All that hard work getting an appointment with a potential client. You make a good pitch and agree to follow it up with a quotation. This is one of the most important tools in your promotion and sales kit and you just run off something boring and lifeless!

Why? How about adapting this version used by a small builder?

Dear Mrs Harvey,

Thank you for requesting a quotation for xxxxxxxxx [the supply of, the repair of].

Following our meeting with you on the xxxxx where you outlined your requirements, the price to carry out xxxxxx is £xxx [plus VAT or not?].

As a client you will be automatically subject to the following guarantees.

• All the materials and equipment required to carry out this work are included in the price — there are no extras.
• The work will be carried out at a time and date convenient to you. If you have a deadline we will do our best to work closely with you to meet it.
• If we are late in arriving, the bill will be reduced by 5%.
• The workplace will be left clean and tidy and all rubbish will be removed.
• You will be contacted periodically to check that the work carried out is still providing you with the level of service required.
• If you are not completely satisfied with

the standard of our work your decision is final and you will be entitled to request a refund.

I will contact you in two working days to discuss this quotation and look forward to the opportunity of helping you to achieve xxxxxx (a reduction in your overhead, a more efficient system - remember to highlight the main benefit to them!).

Yours sincerely

Guarantee
If you really believe that your business is second to none, then mean it and say it. Put your money where your mouth is:

Our Sandwiches Are The Best
How about this one used by a sandwich shop?
'No Quibble Guarantee – We guarantee that if you are not completely satisfied with the quality of your sandwich and our service, we will replace the sandwich or give you a full refund.'

News Releases
News Release is the correct name for what you and I call a Press Release.

Your local paper doesn't have a huge team of journalists hunting down stories. It depends on readers to feed it news. But don't just ring the editor and waffle on about how wonderful you are – you need to be more methodical. Send them a press – whoops, sorry, news – release. It needs structuring and here are the ground rules to follow to avoid getting yours thrown in the bin – as over 80 per cent are!

• Key questions they want answering are: What? Why? When? How? Where? Who?

- Find out to whom you need to send the news release; identify the journalist who covers your subject.
- **AJAMA**: Avoid Jargon And Meaningless Acronyms – like that! Keep it simple.
- Don't blatantly advertise; journalists hate this and you will get their backs up. Newspapers are only interested in *stories* that revolve around *people*. Telling them about the technical specifications of your new machine will get your release filed in the bin. Instead, angle it around people – how will the new machine make things better for your workers or customers?
- Find out their time scale and deadlines.
- Print it on good quality stationery. Put **NEWS RELEASE** in bold near the top. Date it and add **FOR IMMEDIATE RELEASE**. Add your full name and contact details.
- Use a simple and clear headline and type in double spacing with wide margins.
- You'll find with double spacing that by the time you've included the header material your main copy may start halfway down the first side of A4. The overrun should take up no more than another side – you're not Microsoft.
- Always include a quote from yourself, one of your staff and/or from a credible third party. Add a note to the top stating that you are available for interview.
- Write in a newspaper style: 'James Smith, 7, said of Carter's Lollipop Factory. . .'. Remember to use the third person rather than the first – 'he, she, it' rather than 'I, we, us'.
- Put **ENDS** after the last paragraph. Add **Photo Opportunity** – and contact details, or list a web address where they can find high definition images for immediate use.

When it is printed, copy it and use it to circulate to prospective clients. Keep the press informed about milestones in your business – the thousandth customer, etc.

So there you have it. Some ideas on how to promote your business.

Remember, no matter what stage your business is at: **keep, keep, keep promoting!**

7

RUNNING THE BUSINESS

There is an often used question by business advisers. 'Are you running your business, or is it running you?' Clever or what? You see why they are advisers now. Remember those things that finance people keep going on about: cash flow, profit and loss, break-even, pricing structure? Well, this is where they start to come into their own. Simply put, they tell you if your business idea is working or not. After you have been running your business for a while you can start filling in the real figures in your previously Gypsy Rose Lee projections. And guess what? They won't match. If they do, then you have either made a pact with the devil or you *are* Gypsy Rose Lee. So why bother to do the projections in the first place? Targets, set yourself targets – enough said!

Meeting
An event where minutes are taken and hours wasted.
James C Kirk

Well the first rule for running your business is: **get paid!** Truth is it might as well be the only rule. In that case this is going to be a short chapter and we can all go home early. But, no, there are a few other things that you need to get on top of, and we shall come to them later. But back to the 'get paid' one, I have seen (with horror) businesses continue to supply their 'best customer' despite this 'best customer' having not paid them for months. Now, is that really your 'best customer'? Or are they taking the you-know-what? 'But I may lose their business if I chase too hard for payment.' OK, then lose your business instead, because that is where it is heading. They will just find another sucker supplier. Get your terms and conditions clear from the outset with any new customer.

In the Appendix you will find listed under Better Payment a website which provides plenty of excellent guidance and downloadable letters. Use them!

Make it Clear From Day One

Make Your Terms Clear...
I know one consultant who has the following terms and conditions:
Invoice due in 14 days.
Failure to comply will result in:
Day 15 – a phone call to you . . . and
Day 16 – you see me.
Simple but effective!
These terms are made abundantly clear before any work is agreed between him and a client – who then has to sign a document agreeing to them.

Early Settlement Incentives . . .
Perhaps offer your customers an early settlement discount – but make sure you have it covered in your pricing to them. Speedy settlement by your debtors will help to keep your cash flow positive.

Add Interest for Late Payment . . .
Tricky one this. I would advocate it but not many people on either side of this arrangement appear to invoke it.

> **Insanity**
> There is nothing that is a more certain sign of insanity than to do the same thing over and over again and expect the results to be different.
> *Albert Einstein*

Business Skills

The running your business bit is all about business skills. In Chapter 1 we looked at your personal skills. But business skills need to run in tandem with your wonderful personal talents. So what business skills do we need?

In a typical day I reckon I will use the following skills:

Receptionist
Meet and greet clients and ask if they want a coffee.

Telephonist
Make appointments with clients.

Chief Buyer
Buy my stationery, etc.

Office Supervisor
Keep my office ticking over.

Cleaner
Wash the car and keep the desk tidy.

IT Manager
Oh this one keeps me going all right!

PR
Keep the local press fed with stories.

Stores Manager
Keep the stationery in order.

Head of Accounts
Do the books and pay.

Marketing Supremo
Come up with ways to promote, then become . . .

Head of Advertising
Place the adverts.

Sales Manager
Get the business.

Customer Service Supremo
Look after the blighters.

Training Manager
Keep myself up-to-date.

Catering Manager
Make my sandwiches.

I think you get the drift!

Get An Expert
Is Your Time Better Spent Elsewhere?
A jewellery maker I was working with rang me up one morning to tell me that she was very concerned with her book-keeping.

'Oh dear, what is the problem?'

'I can't make it balance. It's a real worry. I started yesterday afternoon and it just won't add up.'

'How much are you out?' I asked.

'I'm £16 out somewhere,' she replied.

She had spent an afternoon, a sleepless night, most of the next morning trying to sort out £16!

'Do you have customers waiting for jewellery?'

'Oh yes – loads of them.'

'Then get a book-keeper!'

Why waste time on something you are poor at in business whilst neglecting what you are good at?

She got herself a book-keeper!

Incidentally, I thought she would struggle to make something of her business. I am so glad that she proved me wrong!

Be honest: you can't be good at everything so get yourself trained. Or use the services of someone else to fill the gap and leave yourself free to get on with what you are good at; book-keeping is something most of us hate, so get someone to take it on and leave yourself free to sell or make your product.

Committee
A group of people who individually can do nothing but as a group decide nothing can be done.
Fred Allen

Discounting

Now more about that darn discounting topic. As was pointed out to me by a tame accountant, if you can prove that your product or service is very sensitive to a price change then a reduction may increase profits but in general the price may be less sensitive than expected.

Convenience, habit, previous satisfaction, quality concerns, and even 'better the devil you know' can make customers reluctant to switch allegiances for the sake of a few pence.

Remember:

Increasing sales by cutting prices may boost turnover but hits your profit.

There is a finance saying:

Turnover is vanity – profit is sanity – but cash is reality!

On occasion you may be able to prove lower prices generate higher profits – but would an increase in the number of items you sell be realistic?

Creditors
The creditors hath a better memory than the debtor.
James Howell

Words and Expressions the Self-Employed Should NEVER Use

There is a saying that there are three types of people in this world.

- Those that make it happen.
- Those that watch it happen.
- Those that say 'what happened?'

Which are you? Or more important – which category do you think the self-employed should belong to? I say 'should' because far too many are in the wrong category.

On the same thread there are some words and expressions the self-employed should never be heard using. For example:

'Not my fault' you bleat as your customer asks why you are two hours late arriving at his premises. Problems with suppliers are no concern to your customer. This is your business so keep on top of it.

'If only . . .' you had seen that potential customer or got that quote out on time. No place for 'if only' in the world of the self-employed. Remember that when you started you wanted to be in control of your own destiny.

Organisation

Of course a major factor in running your business is organisation. And the best tool to help you with this is: a diary.

Keep one to log contacts and plan ahead. I don't care if it is a full blown PDA or a basic old-fashioned paper-based diary, just use one! If you are disorganised, then you will quickly lose business to your competitors; it is as simple as that.

List things as either Must Do or Could Do and do the Must Do's first.

Paperwork

This includes the dreaded book-keeping. Keep on top of it. I remember one client who was convinced that if he tore bills up they went away! If you are useless at paperwork, get help – it will release you to take care of other parts of your business. And you don't need fancy software to do your book-keeping; a straightforward paper-based system will be fine. The days of going into work and pretending to be busy, whilst watching the clock, are gone!

Travel

Mileage – at the time of writing, if you are doing under 10,000 business miles a year you will probably be better off charging the business 40p per business mile in your vehicle. If you use a bike you can charge the business 20p a mile! An accountant will advise you and show you how to log it and then claim against tax.

Ten Top Tips

Never Over Promise

Be honest with your customers. Don't be a delivery optimist. Also, learn to say NO if you can't do something, rather than let customers down.

Don't Buy It

Try to balance being a skin flint with looking good in business. Er, what? Well, question every purchase and maybe you can borrow or rent the equipment – but never pay for it outright. Hang on to cash!

Save for Your Tax Bill

Open an ISA account, buy Premium Bonds but save for that tax bill. In Chapter 8, there is an example of how much you may have to pay in tax, per your level of profit.

Take Care of Your Customers

I know it is harping on again but make yourself stand out from the crowd – treat your customers properly. Without them you are not in business. Simple.

Check Out New Customers

While you want to get credit terms from your suppliers, apply this principle in reverse when it comes to a new customer you are not sure about. Ask for trade references and, if they are a new business and cannot provide them, ask for money upfront or a deposit. This is all part of a key business skill – negotiation.

Keep Looking for New Clients

Always be on the look-out for new clients – particularly when you have current clients. There is some strange law about them being easier to find when you are successful. I think it is because the successful business person exudes confidence.

Don't Mix the Pub and Business

What you can't go to the pub again? Well of course you can, just remember why you went there – to switch off! If a client were to ring you and they can tell you are in the pub, how professional does that background noise sound to them?

Avoid Whingers

Don't moan and avoid moaners. Your destiny is in your own hands. Some small business owners will find all sorts of reasons for lack of work – but never blame themselves. And don't moan with your customers. Try to be positive. If you are not happy in business, get out of it!

Take Time Off

Relax, switch off if you can. Hmm – this is one I can be guilty of not doing. Better listen to myself at this bit. You can get so engrossed you forget about the family and friends: don't. They are important.

Reward Yourself

Hang on a minute, you said further back about being a skin flint. Now, you are telling me to reward myself. Well, little rewards then. When you were employed you may have received the occasional bonus. It's the same principle: you deserve the odd reward. You could say if I get a certain client then I will treat myself to a new xxxxxx – you deserve it!

What if it All Goes Wrong and I Fail in Business?
Fair question.

Well, first of all, never be afraid to keep questioning the progress of your business. Don't be stubborn, review it with an accountant, adviser, somebody, anybody.

You may be under-capitalised, have cash-flow problems, bad debts, poor management skills or a limited customer base. But this is your business – identify the problem and do something about it!

David Quayle (the 'Q' in B&Q stores) had a pottery business which ran into trouble. He says you have to know when to get out and be prepared to take the blame for your mistakes. 'It was your idea and you must be prepared to accept the blame.' Harsh words? Well, probably the most dangerous person to go into business is one who doesn't know how to lose.

Top entrepreneurs don't do blame – they learn from their mistakes. And, if you have the bug for self-employment, you may well try another venture.

You will have acquired new skills and, after recovering from your stumble, you may want to try again!

8

FAQS: A COLLECTION OF 'WHAT ABOUT?' QUESTIONS

FAQs are great. They can mop up the bits that my brain has forgotten. They are listed randomly but comprise some of the most often asked questions by start-ups. Invariably they will start with 'What about...' Hence the chapter title.

What about a Form of Trading?
There are seven ways in which you can structure your business:

- Sole Trader (i.e. just good old you!).
- Partnership (minimum of two people).
- Limited Liability Partnership.
- Company Limited by Guarantee.
- Private Limited Company.
- Public Limited Company (not a common option for a start-up business).
- Co-Operative.

Limited Liability Partnership (LLP) is a relatively new form of trading in the UK: It offers those setting up a partnership the flexibility to operate as a partnership, while the liability of the partners can be limited. LLPs register details with Companies House, file annual accounts, and notify them of any changes to members' details and addresses.

Partners will still be subject to the same tax system for a traditional partnership. The main benefits of the new status appear to be greater protection from personal bankruptcy, protection from fraud by another partner and the tax situation. LLP status does not require partners to pay National Insurance as an employer and employee. To register as an LLP currently costs £14 (electronically) or £40 (on paper). More information is available on the Companies House website. See the Appendix for details.

Partnerships

Partnerships should draw up a Deed of Partnership. This will show how profits will be shared (and any losses!). And cover the retirement, or withdrawal of one of the partners, should they decide to split up. Without a Deed of Partnership, profits (or losses) would be shared equally. A solicitor's advice should be used to draw up the agreement.

Partnerships formed between friends can be likened to a marriage, and sadly not all run to plan, so be prepared and try to anticipate any problems. Clearly define the role and responsibilities of each partner. Cynics even advise clarifying when holidays are taken!

Limited Liability Company

In law, a limited liability company is a legal entity in its own right and so it can be sued. The owners (shareholders) are liable only for any amount of remaining unpaid shares for which they have subscribed, hence the term 'limited liability'. However, if the owners need to borrow to start the business they will probably have to personally guarantee any loans. An accountant or solicitor can incorporate your company. Also agents specialising in company formation can be found in magazines like *Exchange & Mart*, and they can provide you with an 'off-the-shelf' limited company for about £120.

Some clients expect to deal with a limited company,

believing they are dealing with a 'proper' business, and currently there can be tax advantages; an accountant can advise you in the light of your individual background. Sole traders and partnerships are taxed at individual rates, but a limited company is subject to corporation tax. Bear in mind that you will have to file audited accounts and the directors (owners) of a limited company are subject to rigorous legal obligations. It's not as onerous as it can sound, though.

Sole Traders and Timing the Tax Trading Year

If it isn't too important when your tax year runs, it will be much easier for you if you run with the same one as HMRC – in effect, April to March the following year.

You will find it so much easier to compile your self-assessment tax forms, as these dates coincide with them.

However, if March is not a quiet year end because you are too busy for a stock take, for example, then pick dates that suit you.

What about Registering a Business?

There is much confusion with this requirement when starting up a business. Often start-ups will ask: 'How do I register my business?' If you intend to trade as a sole trader or partnership, you do not need to register a business name. However, if you decide to form a limited company you must register the business with Companies House.

As a sole trader, the only form of 'registering' the business is when you tell the HMRC.

Don't Get Fined

You must now register as self-employed, within three months of starting your own business. You can register online via the HMRC website. A start-up pack will also be sent to you, detailing how to handle your National Insurance payments, etc. Ironically, the pack has a red tape around it which needs cutting before you can get at the contents inside. The HMRC has either a sense of irony or used the services of a marketing consultant. Failure to inform HMRC will result in a £100 fine – you have been warned!

What about Accounts?

In business it is important to keep proper books and records. If you are trading as a limited company the book-keeping and administration must meet the requirements of the Companies Act. Choose your accounting year to suit your type of business and try to coincide your year-end accounts with a quiet period. This will give you time to carry out related tasks like stock-taking. Your accounting year need not coincide with the 'tax year' or run from the beginning of January to the end of December!

Changes under self-assessment taxation have made things easier for sole traders (honestly) but if you have any questions contact your local tax office and consult an accountant. To source an accountant, ask around locally or check in Yellow Pages – always get a quote first before committing yourself to their services.

Accountant
A man hired to explain that you didn't make the money you thought you did.
Maxim Drabon

Limited companies will need to file audited accounts and will require the services of a good accountant. Even if you plan to use a book-keeper, it probably isn't a bad idea to attend a book-keeping course at a local college. At least you can grasp the principles and have an idea if your book-keeper is competent or not!

But, if your talents and skills are in other areas of running the business, why waste a day a week or so on book-keeping when your time could be better served selling or manufacturing?

What Expenses Can I Claim Against My Tax in the UK?

Employee Costs
Salaries, bonuses, casual wages, pension contributions.

Premises
Rent, rates, utilities, insurance, security, and don't forget the use of home.

Repairs
To property, renewals, maintenance.

General Administration Expenses
Phone, fax, mobile, stationery, print, postage, computer costs, subscriptions, insurance.

Motoring
Fuel, servicing, repairs, insurance, parking, RAC/AA membership.

Entertainment
Staff only or customer gift up to £50 that advertises your business.

Advertising and Promotion
Trade shows, mail shots, samples, brochures.

Legal and Professional
Accountancy, legal, architects.

Bad Debts
Interest on overdraft, bank loans and other loans.

Other Finance Charges
Bank charges, HP, credit card charges, leasing.

Depreciation
See – you do need to consult an accountant!

What about Registering a Business Name?

The Business Names Register was abolished several years ago. You can trade under your own name and, as it is not classed as a 'business name', registration is not required. If you use a business name, you should check that it is not in use already. You could face legal action if you are found 'passing off' a business name already in use. For example, only a fool would use Macdonald's for a fast food business!

If you form a limited company, a check is done automatically and you can always ring Companies House and check if the name is in use. Unfortunately, they can only advise you about limited companies and not sole traders or partnerships trading under a business name. So, get yourself to the local library. Check in Yellow Pages and business directories. If your chosen name appears to be available, then you must draw up a letterhead and state on your paperwork who any partners are, etc. It must be abundantly clear to the world just who is behind this business!

Can you protect the name? Difficult, but lodge a copy of your details with a solicitor and then if you face a legal battle they will at least have a date when you established your business name. In the UK you could also consider using the Business Names Register. See the Appendix for details.

Also, think long and hard about a business name from a marketing point of view. Your name will sum you up, either good or bad, to your clients so choose carefully!

What about Taxation, National Insurance and VAT?

Big changes were made to the taxation system for the self-employed when self-assessment was introduced.

Self-Assessment Taxation
The best mail order business in the world.
Anon

Directory Enquiries

In the UK the phone directory enquiries services can be a useful way of finding out if a business name is in use or not.

If you say the name of the business but can't remember which town it is in, Directory Enquiries will perform a national search.

You can also check them on the different directory enquiries websites and by using different search engines.

Note the numbers, ring them. Ask them what they do and, if it is the same type of business you are about to launch, change your proposed name and try again!

As soon as you become self-employed inform the local Revenue & Customs office, whose contact details can be found in your local phone directory. Get hold of their booklet called 'Are you thinking of working for yourself?', number P/SE/1. This booklet has some good practical tips and the form that you fill out to inform the authorities (i.e. tax, National Insurance, and VAT) that you are now of self-employed status.

Back in the days when you were employed, deductions were taken care of by your employer. Remember that you are now about to undergo a big change in emphasis when it comes to payment of tax. It will no longer be deducted as you earn it, under PAYE (Pay As You Earn). You will need to set aside funds to pay tax and be ready for the bill when it arrives. National Insurance payments can be paid monthly but your tax liability will be retrospective – so be ready for it!

Taxation

In some respects the payment of tax isn't such a bad thing (seriously!). After all, to have a tax liability does mean that your business has made something. So while you grudgingly collect taxes via VAT and PAYE for the Government, console yourself with that thought. Businesses assist the Government in collecting tax through the PAYE and the VAT system. To understand the system properly you will need to get yourself a good accountant, and he will explain the workings of the Revenue. He will also keep you up-to-date about current tax rates and allowances. For example, at the time of writing you can claim 50 per cent of the cost of IT equipment for your business!

The tax year runs from the 6th of April in one year until the 5th of April in the following year. As I stated earlier, in business you are not obliged to run your year to coincide with these dates. Choose dates convenient to you and your business and try to have your year-end at a quiet time – oh yes, you will get them!

Payment will be influenced by the form of business you will be trading as. So, a sole trader will be liable for all the tax due on the profit made by his or her business; whereas in a partnership the profit is shared according to the split as defined in the partnership agreement (please draw one up!) and consequently so is the tax liability. Don't forget that your personal allowances will also influence, up or down, the amount of taxation due. You will be taxed on the total profits made by the business before you take your wages (called 'drawings' in financial parlance).

Now we have mentioned one financial term 'drawings' perhaps defining some others may be useful at this stage – so here goes!

Free Courses

In the UK your local tax office will run some *free* courses about:

Self-Assessment Tax
Setting up a Limited Company
Employing Staff
National Insurance

Find their number in your local phone book. You have no excuse now!

'Capital' and 'Revenue' Expenditure and a bit on 'Depreciation'
In business, expenditure is split as either capital or revenue expenditure. Capital expenditure covers the assets like office equipment, machinery, and vehicles. As these items need to be replaced every so often, you can deduct depreciation from your profits. Depreciation cannot be claimed towards your taxable profits and you, your accountant and the tax authorities will agree on your depreciation figure – so, get a good accountant!

However, your capital expenditure is allowed a capital allowance. From 6th April 2012, for a figure of £25,000 or above, different criteria applies. The rest of us (i.e. below £25,000) should qualify for an 18 per cent capital allowance against the first year from 6th April 2012.

N.B. Please check all figures and rates quoted with your local tax office.

After your revenue expenditure and capital allowances are deducted from your income, the balance is classed as your profit and subject to tax.

Revenue expenditure such as materials, overheads, wages for employees and allowable business expenses are deducted from income in order to arrive at net profit.

Self-Assessment
There is a rigid timetable to follow under this system! Briefly it is as follows:

In April you will be sent a letter telling you to complete your tax return. If you choose to fill in a paper return, you must send it to HMRC to arrive by 31st October. If you choose to fill in your tax return online (which is recommended by HMRC), the figures are calculated automatically and you'll know straightaway what tax you owe.

Either way, you must pay any tax due by 31st January. You will also need to pay a further payment by 31st July against your next tax bill. Be warned – miss either of these dates and there are fines waiting for you.

Employees

If you employ anyone under PAYE you deduct income tax and National Insurance from their earnings and forward this amount to the Government.

Corporation Tax

Should your business be a limited company registered with Companies House then it will pay Corporation Tax due on the calculated profit the business makes. The individual directors of the company pay tax under the PAYE system just like any other employees of a business. They also draw 'dividends' – see, you really do need an accountant!

Check the current rates of Corporation Tax. The small companies' rate from 1st April 2012 is 20 per cent up to profits of £300,000. All Corporation Tax returns now have to be done online. You probably need an accountant.

National Insurance

The Inland Revenue and the agency dealing with National Insurance Contributions merged a few years ago. Which confirmed what we all knew, of course – that NI is another form of taxation!

National Insurance contributions count towards the following benefits: pension, unemployment benefit and incapacity benefit. Payments are compulsory and can be topped up by voluntary payments. Like tax, there are fines for non-payment. It may be worth getting a pension forecast from The Pension Service (see the Appendix) and finding out just what your payment will be in the future.

You can come under one or more of the NI classes depending on whether you employ someone or not.

There are two classes of National Insurance that affect the self-employed:

Class 2 Contributions

Class 2 National Insurance is paid by all self-employed people, whether sole traders or partners. The current rate is £2.50 a week. 'Not bad,' I hear you shout. But wait – this is not the end of the story.

Class 4 Contributions
Class 4 National Insurance is also paid by the self-employed – but this one is based on your profits made above £7,225 up to £42,475. See, it is another form of tax! The current rate is 9 per cent.

Should you decide to take on an employee, then you will also be responsible for:

Class 1 Contributions
Class 1 National Insurance relates to the employed and are paid by both the employer and employee. You will be responsible for paying both contributions, deducting the employees' contributions through the PAYE scheme.

NB Please check all figures and rates quoted with your local HMRC office.

How much tax will I pay?
At the time of writing (assuming a standard personal allowance) the following figures show approximately how much money you may need to set aside to meet your tax and Class 4 National Insurance bill when it becomes due in the UK

Estimated Net Profit (£ per month)	Approx. Amount to Set Aside (£ per month)
700	25
1,000	110
1,200	170
3,000	700

Please remember: the correct liability cannot be calculated until a completed tax return is filed with HMRC

Value Added Tax (VAT)

VAT is taxed on most products or services – though not all, for example, education and training, and postal services are exempt. If items are taxable there are three rates:

- Standard (20 per cent).
- Reduced (5 per cent).
- Zero Rated (0 per cent).

Exempt items are not the same as zero-rated items by the way. Good fun this one, isn't it?

Your VAT payments are usually made each quarter to HM Revenue & Customs. It's only necessary to register if business activities through your sales are taxable, and you must currently register for VAT if your annual turnover is over £73,000.

Consider voluntary registration when you start up, because the VAT paid on purchases can be reclaimed. You can also reclaim VAT on capital equipment, materials, and stocks bought before registration. Always seek advice from an accountant to check if your business should register. If you are VAT-registered you are expected to show your registration number on your invoices and business stationery.

VAT

As a rough guide:

If your business deals with the public then try to avoid having to charge VAT. You will in effect be putting your prices up by 20 per cent.

If you will be dealing with other businesses, then VAT will probably not concern them too much.

Also bear in mind that you cannot wait until you reach that £73,000 figure – you need to assess the situation and if your sales turnover is steady at £1,400 a week you will probably need to register.

There are many useful websites for tax and budget information, including HM Revenue & Customs' own website (see the Appendix.) Most of the main accountancy practices produce Budget Briefings that summarise the main points and implications of Budget Statements. The address of your local tax office can be found in the telephone directory.

Tax Inspector
A person that follows you into a revolving door but comes out ahead of you.
Colin Bowles

What about Business Insurance?

Insurance is often an area where new businesses try to skimp and hope to save money – sometimes they even don't bother to take it out. Sadly, insurance is important but doesn't appear important until it is needed – by which time it is too late! Worse still, there are some forms of insurance that are required by law when starting or running a business. Let's look at these first. You may be surprised to learn that this does not include the one that everybody thinks is a legal requirement.

Motor Insurance
As soon as you start in business, contact your motor insurance company. Not only is this cover required by law, you run the risk of invalidating your cover if you don't inform the insurance firm. Depending on your type of business activity, your premium may not alter. So, check with your insurers – now!

Employers' Liability Insurance
This is compulsory if you employ somebody with a contract of employment. You must have adequate cover against risks caused by their employment with you.

Public Liability Insurance
This covers your legal liability against injury or damage to

third parties, or their property, as a result of the activities of your business, or due to negligence by one of your employees. Apparently, it's not required in law in the UK. Strange but true!

Product Liability

If you manufacture a product and a defect in your product causes injury or damage to third parties, product liability should cover your liability and costs in the event of legal action.

Fire Insurance

You may need to cover business assets such as premises, stock or equipment.

Business Interruption Following Fire

While a fire policy protects the business in the event of loss or damage to the assets, the time taken to replace equipment or stock, plus continuing overheads and loss of income etc., will adversely affect your trading.

Money

A money or cash in transit policy can be arranged to cover cash in transit to or from the business premises or while on your premises.

Theft

Covers the business equipment against loss by theft.

Fidelity

Insurance against losses caused by dishonest employees.

Credit Insurance

Cover against clients who fail to pay!

Goods in Transit

Insuring stock or products against loss or damage whilst in transit.

Engineering Insurances
The Factories Acts require certain items of plant to be inspected by a 'competent' engineer. This covers the danger to third parties by machinery.

Personal Accident and Sickness
Insurance arranged for an employer on a personal basis, or Employee Schemes where the employer wishes to provide 'fringe' benefits for the employees.

Professional Indemnity Insurance
If you give advice to customers and if there is a risk of that advice having a damaging effect on their business.

All of the above are required only because you are in business. But there is one more you need to consider that is very important and personal to you:

Permanent Health Insurance
Self-employed people whose income would cease if they were unable to work should seriously consider this type of insurance. How would you survive if you fell ill?

Where to get business insurance?
Talk to your bank or an insurance broker and make sure you get adequate cover for your business.
   The premiums can be paid by monthly instalments to help your cash flow. Plus the premium is a permitted business expense against tax.

What about the Data Protection Act?
The DPA affects any business that stores personal data about people – you must register. Though if the information is to be used purely for your own marketing purposes, you could be exempt. But check with the Information Commissioner's Office. Address details are in the Appendix.

What about Local Authority Legislation and Licences?

Generally a licence is not required for shops – with some exceptions below. Though if 'change of use' is involved, advice should be sought from your local Planning Department. Also, never assume if you are buying a café, for example, that you can continue to trade in a similar manner. Shop premises have to comply with the Offices, Shops and Railway Premises Act 1963, as amended by the Health and Safety at Work Act 1974. If employees other than the proprietor's immediate family work on the premises, registration with your local Environmental Health Department is required. Your local authority regulates hours of shop opening.

Lawyers for Business

In the UK there is a service run by the Law Society whereby you can get *free* time with a business lawyer. Generally, the time available is about 30 minutes so have your questions prepared in advance!

When seeking legal advice, ask the firm of solicitors if they operate under the Lawyers for Business Scheme.

Local inspectors will enforce these regulations – so make friends with them!

Here are some example licence requirements.

Acupuncture
Licence required from local authority.

Auction Salesroom/Auctioneer
No licence required.

Betting Shops & Agencies
Licence required from your local Magistrates' Court.

Billiard and Snooker Halls
Licence required from your local Magistrates' Court.

Café
No licence required, but Environmental Health Department of local authority must be informed – see Catering below.

Caravan Sites or Camp Sites
Licence required from local authority.

Car Hire
Consumer Hire licence required, this is available from the Office of Fair Trading (OFT).

Catering
All food businesses are required to be 'registered' with the Local Authority (Environmental Health Department) and new businesses by the letter of the regulations should register 28 days before first trading. See page 152.

Children's Nursery
Registration with the Social Services Department of the local authority required.

Conveyancing
Licence required; an application should be made to the Council for Licensed Conveyancers.

Credit
Consumer Credit Licence required before goods can be offered on credit terms. Available from the Office of Fair Trading.
　　Did you know, it is a criminal offence to supply credit without a licence, including sums under £30?

Dating Agency
No licence required.

Dog Kennels
Licence required from the Environmental Health Department of the local authority.

Door-to-Door Selling
See Pedlar's Licence.

Ear Piercing
Licence required from local authority.

Employment Agencies
Licence required from the local Employment Agencies Licensing Office of the Department for Work and Pensions. Certified midwives and qualified nurses also require a licence from the local authority.

Fireworks
Licence required from the local authority.

Food
Manufacturers of food must be licensed by the Environmental Health Department of the local authority, including any catering carried out from home.

Food Shops
See the previous details for 'Catering'.

Guard Dogs
Licence required from the local authority.

Fruit Machines
Licence required from the local authority.

Hairdressers
Licence required by some local authorities, check with your local council.

Hire Purchase
Consumer Credit Licence required before Hire Purchase terms can be offered, this is available from the OFT.

Hypnotherapy
Check with your local authority.

Leasing Out of Goods
Consumer Credit Licence required from the OFT.

Liquor
Licence required from the local Magistrates' Court for anyone
wanting to sell liquor.

Loans/Money
Consumer Credit Licence required from the OFT.

Market Stalls
Are allocated by the Market Superintendent at your local
authority. If selling food, you may also have to comply with
the Food Hygiene Regulations Act 1966 and the Office, Shops
and Railway Premises Act.

Massage Parlours
Licence required from the local authority.

Mobile Food Vans
Food Act 1984 and Food Hygiene (Market Stall and Delivery
Vehicles) Regulations 1966 apply. Most mobile food vans
require a licence or registration with the local Environmental
Health Department and in town centres a Street Traders'
Licence will probably be needed.

Movement of Animals
Licence required from the local authority.

Music
To use music on business premises – hairdressers, etc. –
permission is required from the Performing Rights Society.

Nursing Homes
Registration required with the Social Services Department of
the local authority.

Party Plan
The sale of goods by means of parties given by people in their own homes may be subject to the provisions of the Shops Act 1950. Check with your local authority in case there are any statutory requirements.

Pedlar's Licence
Required for door-to-door selling and is issued by the local police station.

Performing Animals
Licence required from the local authority.

Pet Shops
Licence required from the Environmental Health Department of the local authority.

Petrol
Licence required from the local authority.

Pharmaceuticals
If dealing in wholesale pharmaceuticals a licence is required from the Medicines and Healthcare Products Regulatory Agency. See the Appendix.

Pleasure Boats
Licence required from the local authority.

Postage Stamps
Other than at post offices, the sale of postage stamps is permissible, but must be authorised by the Post Office, which provides a certificate of authorisation for display.

Private Car Hire
Licence required from the local authority.

Renting Out Goods
Consumer Hire Licence required from the OFT.

Restaurants
Licence required from the Environmental Health Department of the local authority. Also a Table Licence and a Liquor Licence may be required from your local Magistrates' Court.

Riding Schools
Licence required from the local authority.

Scrap Metal Dealers
Licence required from the local authority.

Sex Shops
Licence required from the local authority.

Street Traders
Licences usually required in town centres. Contact your local Environmental Health Department.

Taxi
Licence required from the local authority.

Television Dealers/Repairers
Contact the Dealer Section at the TV Licensing Office in Bristol.

Theatre
Licence required from the local authority.

Wild Animals
Licence required from the local authority.

NB. This list is not complete and each council can have some local requirements that you need to comply with, so check with your local Trading Standards Office.

What about Premises?

After salaries or drawings, premises costs could be the next highest overhead for most small businesses, so it is vital that you make the right decision.

Consider how much you can afford to pay. Build the cost of premises into your cash-flow forecast. It is important that you do not take occupation of premises in the faint hope that the profits you will make will cover your premises costs – you have heard the expression 'Well, as long as the premises pay for themselves . . .'

Where to Find Business Premises
Help in locating premises is often available through local authorities. Check with the Business or Economic Development section within your local council and ask if they keep a 'property database'. This will save you a lot of legwork with estate agents, as this database will list all vacant property in the area.

Location is important for your business. Do you need to be in the centre of town, or in a unit on the outskirts? Is it difficult for your customers and suppliers to get to you?

Make a checklist of what you need. Include access, security, parking and other services that are important to your business.

Be Certain You Know the Following
- How much is the rent? How often is it increased?
- How is the rent paid? And how frequently?
- How much are the rates and who is responsible for paying them?
- Are there service charges?
- What period of notice is required from either side to quit?
- Is there a deposit? How much is it? Is it refundable?
- Who is responsible for the repair and redecoration of the premises? Do you have to bring the premises back to their original condition before you leave?

Before you sign an agreement for commercial premises, consult a solicitor.

> **Solicitor**
> A man who calls in a person he doesn't know to sign a contract he hasn't seen to buy property he doesn't want with money he hasn't got.
> *Dingwall Bateson*

What about Working From Home?

Increasingly, more and more start-ups are based from home. Overheads such as rent and travel are much lower when working from home than renting premises. While starting up it is important to keep costs down. Premises could be considered later as the business grows. However, depending on the type of business you may need planning and part of your home may be liable for business rates – so, check the situation (discreetly!) with your local authority. Using one room or part of a room for an office is unlikely to incur business rates.

Also, bear in mind insurance and mortgage implications – the deeds will usually prohibit you from running a business from home and you may invalidate your home insurance if you do not inform your insurance company! More importantly though, some find working from home a distraction and need to have that physiological feeling of 'going to work'.

If you use one or more rooms of your own house for your business, you may be able to claim a proportion of rent, rates, telephone, heating, lighting, insurance, etc., as a business expense against your tax liability. However, for tax purposes, it may be wise to say that you don't have a dedicated business room. Always say that all rooms are domestic and that you carry out your business activity in any room of your home. Guess what? Speak to that accountant again. Just clarify any capital gains tax issues with your accountant.

What about Business Banking?

There isn't a law that states you must have a business bank account when in business – not yet anyway. But banks frown upon it if you run a business from a private account and, to be

---

Working From Home

Do you really need that office?

Applying the skinflint start-up principle, ask yourself if you can do without that fancy office. I have worked with plenty of clients who use a bedroom or kitchen table as an office.

What if a client wants to meet me but not at their premises?

Well, find yourself a nice hotel to meet him at. Say you are out and about that day and suggest that a convenient place is such-and-such hotel. He will think you are ever so busy and important. It's all smoke and mirrors!

Nowadays you can rent presentation rooms for meetings if you want more priority.

One client worked from a glorified garden shed and he said that his walk to work was important. It was his way of applying discipline to his daily routine. Another client always went out in the morning to buy a daily paper. On returning home, he was 'at work'.

---

honest, if you intend to take your business activity seriously, then a business bank account is a good idea.

Remember: you shouldn't pay any charges for everyday banking activities on the account for a specified period – which could be at least a year. Loans and overdrafts will, of course, incur charges. However, these days you have a greater choice of where to open and run a business bank account. You are no longer limited to the established main high street banks.

Building societies have come up fast on the outside with some attractive business banking packages. So, shop around; remember that they are keen for new business accounts and that deals can be negotiated to suit your requirements much more these days.

Running your business through a separate account will

certainly make HMRC more comfortable about your business dealings! Plus if you are using an accountant he will appreciate this cleaner approach to compiling your tax affairs.

Banking Tips
When you do start to pay bank charges, question them. The bank may base them on your performance record in those early stages. Well, back then you wrote cheques like they were going out of fashion, didn't you? After all, there were no charges to pay. But hang on – now you could be paying about 60 pence a cheque, so rein in that habit right now. How about a business charge card? Then you just write one cheque at the end of the month – while paying off all the card of course! And, yes, we are talking charge card not credit card. Similarly, don't pay in as frequently, again to minimise those charges. How about using the internet more? In the immortal words of Robbie Coltrane 'We are all bank managers now.'

On occasion some banks will offer you a period of free banking as an incentive to introduce a business account to them from one of their competitors. So, when a friend of yours says he is not happy with his business bank, offer to introduce him to your business bank manager!

What about Online Trading?
There are several areas you need to consider when trading online.

Distance Selling
In the UK in 2000 Distance Selling regulations were brought in to protect online buyers. The Consumer Protection (Distance Selling) Regulations 2000 now includes contracts made over the internet. The seller is required to give information about the identity of the supplier, the supplier's address, a description of the main characteristics of the goods, the price, delivery costs, arrangements for payment, delivery and the existence of a right of cancellation. The Regulations allow for cancellation of the contract if notice

in writing (or possibly e-mail) is given within seven days. That period may be extended by three months where the seller fails to give the required information. Where the cancellation period has expired, to obtain a remedy the buyer will be required to show that the goods were different from those he contracted to buy or otherwise not of satisfactory quality. Unless specified otherwise, performance of the contract must take place within 30 days. Exemption to the regulations apply to contracts for the sale of land, contracts relating to financial services, or contracts concluded at auction.

Data Protection

The Data Protection Act 1998 requires anyone processing data relating to a living individual (i.e. personal data) to comply with the Act. If you collect and process data relating to your customers and visitors to your site, the Act will apply.

The Act sets out eight principles:

1. Data must be processed fairly and lawfully.
2. It must be obtained for one or more specified purposes.
3. It must be adequate, relevant and not excessive.
4. It must be accurate and up-to-date.
5. It must be processed in accordance with the rights of data subjects.
6. It must not be kept for longer than is necessary.
7. Appropriate technical and organisational measures must be put in place to ensure its integrity.
8. It must not be transferred without consent.

You need to add a privacy statement to your site identifying what personal data is being collected, why the data is being collected and how it will be used.

The legislation also provides rights to individuals to have access to personal data held about them and a right to prevent processing for the purposes of direct marketing.

Terms and Conditions

Terms and conditions must be considered very carefully when trading online. Your terms and conditions need to be clear about the user's access and use of materials on the site and clear about any online transaction. Remember that your website may be accessed from anywhere in the world. You need to be aware about the issues of which law will apply in the event of a dispute and which courts have jurisdiction. You might include a term limiting the territories into which you are prepared to sell goods or services, particularly if you have concerns about compliance with the laws of certain territories. On sensible sites the buyer will click an 'I accept' button indicating acceptance of the terms and conditions and making it clear when the contract is formed.

Copyright

Your terms and conditions about use of the site should include a statement about ownership of copyright in the site and indicate restrictions on copying or use of the content of the site.

No formal system of copyright registration exists in the UK. Though not a legal requirement, a copyright notice and the symbol © should be on your home page plus the year claimed for copyright. It also shows potential infringers of your copyright that you will defend your rights. Copyright in a website can cover text, photographs, graphics, sound, film and computer programs. And I bet you didn't know this bit – copyright in a site can be infringed by use of a link. So, get consent before linking to a third party site. Also, if you arrange that a third party designs your site, make sure you own copyright in it.

Domain Names

Just like choosing your business name, make sure your chosen domain name is yours to use! Registration of a name which incorporates someone else's trade mark or trade name may give rise to proceedings under the Trade Marks Act 1994 (in the case of a registered mark) or passing off (in the case of an unregistered mark). Consider carrying out a trade mark search. Check, as best you can, by searching the local telephone and trade directories, that the name is not used by another business as an unregistered mark.

eBay

eBay, the auction website, has revolutionized the way some businesses trade. In recent years the number of eBay users has grown to over 7 million in the UK alone. You can very effectively and cheaply reach an enormous market. However, the rules for any start-up still apply: research your potential market and provide a top-class service. On eBay your feedback as a seller is very important and it is vital to get and keep it high.

Another important rule to remember is that the Revenue are watching eBay so you will need to keep good records and register as a business if you intend to do any serious trading on eBay. You can find good tips on how to trade on eBay on their site.

Tax

The best for last! There are tax implications when selling online, and in the UK be warned that the taxman is watching you online. Due to the global nature of e-business it can raise issues with regard to taxation. If your server is located in a country outside the UK you could be subject to that country's tax regime – though this will depend on the taxation laws of that territory and is probably unlikely. If your server is located within the UK but you sell into other countries, it is unlikely that you will be subject to the tax regime of those countries **BUT** check with HMRC.

Useful resources about online trading are given in the Appendix.

9

AND FINALLY

And finally, the ubiquitous tips. While I tend to hate placing business in neat boxes like those wonderful 'top ten tips' you see everywhere, this contribution from other start-ups could help make the difference. So here we go...

Keep asking these questions about yourself and your business – review your answers every month!

- **Keep asking your customers, potential and existing, for their opinions about your product or service.**
  And more importantly learn to take and act on criticism. Never assume you know what they want from you. Ask them and learn.

- **Use your existing customers as your sales force.**
  Find a way to get your customers to pass your details onto their friends. And when they do, thank them with a gift – a bottle of wine for example.

- **Keep saying 'thank you' to your customers.**
  Yes, I know it sounds corny but it goes a long way. It could make you stand out from your competition.

- **What can you do that is different to grab people's attention and make your business stand out from the crowd?**
  How about the builder who always does something, like a bungee jump, for charity every year? The local paper always runs an item and mentions (of course) his business activity.

- **Keep giving the press a news release.**
  Your local press don't have a huge team of journalists, so they depend on you for news.

- **Remember to ASK for the business and avoid finding a reason for delaying asking.**
  It's the fear of 'no' – learn from it. Not everyone is going to want what you are offering. Remember the landscaper that learned from the 'no's'.

- **Maximise every opportunity to promote your business.**
  A client offering secretarial services places one of her flyers in every bit of post she sends out. Why? Well, you never know who opens that envelope – they may know someone who needs that service.

- **Collect and compile a folder of 'good ideas' for inspiration.**
  If you see an advert or flyer you like from another business, punch two holes in it and put it in a folder. Then when you are looking for inspiration you can refer to your collection. That way you become your own ad agency and save loads in fees!

- **Keep checking on your competition.**
  They may have a new angle on your business that you could ride along with.

- **Don't let 'word of mouth' be an excuse for not doing any promotion.**
  Remember that as a start-up you are the mouth that has to create the word.

- **Is there a new trend or legislation that can give your business a new direction?**
  I saw one small builder diversify into chimney sweeping as a result of EU regulations – and did well out of it.

- **What words best describe your product or service? (What is it like? Exciting, special . . .)**
  So make sure your marketing activities and materials are the same – please avoid death by clipart.

- **Remember to keep asking new customers – how did you hear about us?**
That way you will know which forms of promotion are working or not.

- **Never miss an opportunity to sell!**
Always have business cards on you – give them out.

- **Is there an event, exhibition or a related business that can help to raise your profile?**
I saw a mobile chiropodist and gardener link up and distribute each other's cards to their clients – it worked well for them both.

- **Are you getting resistance from potential buyers because they distrust the word 'new'?**
Some of us can be very reluctant to be guinea pigs. Why should I trust it – it isn't proven? Maybe you should try and phrase it how I saw one start-up get around the 'new' word. He changed it to 'after years of research' and lo the orders started to come in.

- **Get paid.**
Remember you are not in business to be a money-lender.

- **And finally – get trained.**
Seek a local organisation running business start-up courses and get on one. 'Well, he is bound to say that isn't he?', I hear you chunter. Yes, OK, as a start-up trainer, I have a vested interest. But I have a bigger interest in seeing people achieve their dreams!

- **So what is your answer to that question at the beginning of the book?**
Which would you rather be employed or self-employed?
Good – then go for it!

START-UP CHECKLIST

Don't panic. Not all of this list will apply to your particular business! Set yourself target dates. Otherwise it is too easy to drift along.

	Target Date	Tick
You		
Aims		
Training		
SWOT		
Legal		
Form of Trading		
Business Name		
Register as Ltd Co		
Name Available		
HM Customs & Excise		
National Insurance		
Local Authority		
Data Protection		
Health & Safety		
Solicitor		

	Target Date	*Tick*
Licences		
Copyright		
Trademarks		
Patents		
Insurance		
Public Liability		
Product Liability		
Motor		
Other		
Premises		
Home		
Planning		
Rates		
Insurance		
Tax		
Neighbours		
Office		
Stationery		
Equipment		
Retail/Workshop		
Location		
Rent/Rates		
Contract		
Get Out Clause		
Access		
Parking		
Security		
Deliveries		

	Target Date	Tick
Banking		
Bank Account		
Free Banking Period		
Charges		
Loan		
Overdraft		
Market Research		
SWOT		
Desk		
Field		
Competition		
Market Size		
Marketing Plan		
Customer Profile(s)		
Price		
Promotion		
Finance		
Starting Capital		
Grants		
Accountant/Book-keeper		
Survival Income		
Overheads		
Sales Forecast		
Profit and Loss		
Cash Flow		
START DATE!		

APPENDIX:
USEFUL CONTACTS
AND WEB LINKS

---

www.startbusiness.co.uk
Start Business's own website with useful information
and links, now managed by Steve's son Aidan.

While most of the following are UK-based they will still
contain useful information wherever you are based.

ACAS: Considering employing someone? Then go to this UK
Government site and find out how to do it properly. Includes
outline statement of employment which you can adapt for
your business: www.acas.org.uk

AP Information Service: Publishers of business directories –
good start for market research: www.apinfo.co.uk

Arts-Based Business: Stacks of information, sourcing arts
grants and fact sheets on running an arts-based business,
setting up an exhibition, etc.: www.arts.org.uk

Ask Cedric: The national one-stop website for all your Trading Standards business-related information: www.askcedric.org.uk/business-index.php

Better Payment: Get paid in other words! UK site with tips and downloadable reminder letters so you can chase up late payers: www.payontime.co.uk

Book-keeping System: Need a simple-to-use and understand book-keeping system? Then this is the publisher for you: www.hingston-publishing.co.uk

British Business Angels Association: The national trade association for the UK's business angel networks and the early stage investment market and is backed by the Department for Business, Enterprise and Regulatory Reform: www.bbaa.org.uk

British Library Business and IP Centre: 96 Euston Road, London, NW1 2DB; www.bl.uk/bipc

British Private Equity and Venture Capital Association (BVCA): www.bvca.co.uk; 020 7025 2950

Business Cards: A very useful website producing competitively priced business cards and leaflets. It also has templates for a very wide range of business types: www.vistaprint.co.uk

Business Funding UK: The UK's most comprehensive directory of business funding websites and other links: www.business-funding-uk.org.uk

Business Gateway (Scotland):
www.bgateway.com; 0845 609 6611

Business Incubation: Business incubation projects, and help for small businesses: www.ukbi.co.uk

Business Insight: One of the best business information libraries in the UK is at Birmingham Central Library: www.birmingham.gov.uk; 0121 303 4531

Business Link: Official UK Government service, providing advice and information for new and small businesses: www.businesslink.gov.uk; 0845 600 9 006

Business Names Register: www.anewbusiness.co.uk

Business Town: Excellent US-based web directory for business ideas and information. Lots of links to resources and tips: www.businesstown.com

Business Wales: http://business.wales.gov.uk; 03000 6 03000 www.anewbusiness.co.uk

Businesses For Sale: Some sites say exactly what they do in their name – and this is one of them. Looking to buy a business? This is the site for you: www.businessesforsale.com

Buying a Business?: Looking to buy an existing business? Then check out Daltons – long-established UK source of businesses for sale: www.daltonsbusiness.com

Catering: For Trading Standards catering information: www.askcedric.org.uk/business-index.php

Companies House: Information about setting up a limited company and a search section to check on business names: www.companieshouse.gov.uk; Companies House, Crown Way, Cardiff, CF14 3UZ; 0303 1234 500

Company Formation UK: Excellent link to form a UK company. Easy to follow online application forms: www.companyregistrations.co.uk

Company Formation US: Provides incorporation services in all 50 states for just $69 plus state fees. Also offers advice on starting up in the US: www.gettingincorporated.com

Data Protection: Be careful – you may need to be registered. Check out the guidelines. Information Commissioner's Office, Wycliffe House, Water Lane, Wilmslow, Cheshire, SK9 5AF; www.ico.gov.uk; 0303 123 1113

Department for Business, Innovation and Skills: The main site for this UK Government department, with links to other Government sites: www.bis.gov.uk

datadepot: Contains *free* information from the area and snap data research sites – some very useful information can be accessed: www.datadepot.co.uk

E-Commerce: www.scottish-enterprise.com; 0845 607 8787

Enterprise Agencies: A UK network of independent, but not for profit, Local Enterprise Agencies targeting pre-start, start-up and micro businesses and assisting in building their ability to survive, to sustain themselves and to grow. Check out which one is near you: www.nfea.com; 01234 831623

Environment: What environmental legislation do you need to be aware of when setting up? Good links on this site: www.envirowise.gov.uk

EU grants: EU site with information on grants:

http://ec.europa.eu/unitedkingdom

Franchising: The British Franchise Association's official website which will help you to make a more informed choice about franchising: www.thebfa.org

Grants: Comprehensive grant information for the UK and Ireland, with over 4,500 financial programmes researched with daily updates, covering European, national Government and lottery funding, plus regional and local funding: www.j4b.co.uk

Health and Safety: What obligations do you face when starting out with regard to health and safety? It makes both common and legal sense to prevent accidents and ill health for you and your employees: www.safestartup.org

HM Revenue & Customs: Not everyone's most favourite subject! Good info for start-ups and covers Tax, VAT and National Insurance contributions: www.hmrc.gov.uk; Employers' Helpline: 0845 7 143 143

Intellectual Property: UK Government-backed site with answers to your questions and all the resources you need to find your way through the IP jungle of Copyright, Designs, Patents and Trade Marks: www.ipo.gov.uk

Instant Search Business Information: Information on UK and international company reports; credit ratings also provided: www.instant-search.com

Kelly's: Well-established source of suppliers: www.kellysearch.co.uk

LearnDirect: Need training for your business? This UK Government online facility is worth checking out: www.learndirect.co.uk

Medicines and Healthcare Products Regulatory Agency: Information Centre, 10-12 Market Towers, 1 Nine Elms Lane, London, SW8 SNQ; www.mhra.gov.uk

MyOwnBusiness: US-based site with plenty of good resources – recommended for US start-ups: www.myownbusiness.org

National Statistics: UK Government site, giving local information, which allows you to find a summary report for your local neighbourhood such as tax bands for housing: www.neighbourhood.statistics.gov.uk

NESTA: No, not the character from the Addams' family. UK independent organisation with help and resources to get that 'better mouse trap' invention up and running: www.nesta.org.uk

Northern Ireland's online business advice service: www.nibusinessinfo.co.uk; 0800 181 4422

Online trading: Useful resources about online trading from Scottish Enterprise: www.scottish-enterprise.com. Also www.tradingstandards. gov.uk (UK official Trading Standards site) and www. ipo.gov.uk (UK official Data Protection Site).

Pension Service: www.direct.gov.uk

PRIME UK: Organisation dedicated to helping people aged over 50 set up in business. Loans may be available for the over-50s to help them start a business: www.primeinitiative.org.uk

The Prince's Trust: Assists 18- to 30-year-olds into business who are unemployed or under-employed (part timers), without the means to start their own business: www.princes-trust.org.uk; 0800 842 842

Professional Contractors Group: The PCG was formed in May 1999 to lobby against the Government's IR35 proposals. It has since evolved from being a single issue group, and its mission is to be recognised as the most effective UK organisation dedicated to protecting and promoting the interests of the freelance community – irrespective of industry focus: www.pcg.org.uk

Star: This site contains facts and figures about tourism in Britain: www.staruk.com

Trading Standards: Official Trading Standards site: www.tradingstandards.gov.uk

UK Trade & Investment: UK Government website with information to help you do business internationally; also guidance for businesses seeking to set up or expand in the UK: www.uktradeinvest.gov.uk

UK Wholesalers Directory: Directory of over 2,300 UK suppliers of a wide range of merchandise: www.ukonlinewholesalers.com

VAT: HM Customs and Excise: www.hmrc.gov.uk

INDEX

To order these Right Way titles please fill in the form below

No. of copies	Title	Price	Total
	Start Your Own Business	£4.99	
	Internet Marketing	£7.99	
	Successful Property Letting	£9.99	
	For P&P add £2.50 for the first book, £1 for each additional book		
	Grand Total		£

Name: _____

Address:_____

_____ Postcode: _____

Daytime Tel. No./Email _____
(in case of query)

Three ways to pay:
1. Telephone the TBS order line on 01206 255 800.
   Order lines are open Monday – Friday, 8:30am–5:30pm.
2. I enclose a cheque made payable to **TBS Ltd** for £_____
3. Please charge my   ☐ Visa   ☐ Mastercard   ☐ Amex
   ☐ Maestro (issue no. _____)

Card number:_____

Expiry date: _____ Last three digits on back of card:_____

Signature: _____

(your signature is essential when paying by credit or debit card)

Please return forms to Cash Sales/Direct Mail Dept.,
The Book Service, Colchester Road, Frating Green,
Colchester CO7 7DW.

Enquiries to readers@constablerobinson.com.

Constable and Robinson Ltd (directly or via its agents)
may mail, email or phone you about promotions or products.

☐ Tick box if you do not want these from us ☐ or our subsidiaries.

www.constablerobinson.com